T H E
Alexander
Plays

ELI

EMERGENT LITERATURES

Emergent Literatures, a series of international scope that makes available, in English, works of fiction that have been ignored or excluded because of their difference from established models of literature.

THE
Alexander
Plays

A D R I E N N E   K E N N E D Y

Foreword by Alisa Solomon

University of Minnesota Press
Minneapolis

Copyright 1992 by Adrienne Kennedy
Foreword copyright 1992 by the Regents of the University of Minnesota

Published by the University of Minnesota Press
2037 University Avenue Southeast, Minneapolis, MN 55414

Library of Congress Cataloging-in-Publication Data

Kennedy, Adrienne.
   The Alexander plays / Adrienne Kennedy : foreword by Alisa Solomon.
     p. cm. — (Emergent literatures)
     Contents: She talks to Beethoven — The Ohio State murders — The film club — The dramatic circle.
     ISBN 0-8166-2077-6 (alk. paper)
     I. Title.   II. Series.
   PS3561.E4252A79   1992
   812'.54—dc20   91-42309
                                         CIP

Printed in the United States of America on acid-free paper
Cover and book design by Patricia M. Boman

2 4 9 1 1 4 2 5

The University of Minnesota is an
equal-opportunity educator and employer.

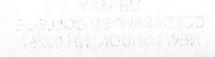
110608

For my sons, Adam and Joe
without whose encouragement
I could not continue to write

Contents

Foreword

Alisa Solomon

In *The Ohio State Murders*, Suzanne Alexander is asked to explain the violent imagery in her work. The play's story, chronicling a dark mystery of kidnapping and infanticide, serves, the character says, as her answer. Of course the answer does not satisfy; the vertiginous world of Adrienne Kennedy's poetic drama resists — indeed, scoffs at — explanation, even when offered by one of its own protagonists.

Since 1964, when *Funnyhouse of a Negro* burst past even the experimental theater's racial, sexual, and formal boundaries, Adrienne Kennedy has been defying the conventions of American play writing to create a new, dangerous, and delirious dramaturgy. From *Funnyhouse* through such plays as *The Owl Answers* (1965), *A Rat's Mass* (1966), *A Lesson in Dead Language* (1970), *A Movie Star Has to Star in Black and White* (1976), and her adaptations of *Electra* (1980) and *Orestes* (1980), Kennedy has been reinventing our notions of character, plot, dialogue, and setting. Her formal experiments continue beyond the stage, as she blurs genre distinctions in her dreamy, scrapbook autobiography, *People Who Led to My Plays* (1987), and, most recently, in *Deadly Triplets* (1990), a mystery-diptych that reflects fiction across nonfiction.

Compared to her earlier plays, those gathered in this volume seem calm, centered. But the omnipresent sense of threat that careened headlong from the previous works—threats to conventional conceptions of race and gender, of culture, and history, of plot, character, and dialogue—lurk in *The Alexander Plays* as well. While these latest works for the stage may not be characterized by the frenetic pitch of, say, *Funnyhouse* or *A Rat's Mass*, they seethe quietly with the same sense of violence and disjuncture, like tranquil waters where reptiles rage hungrily beneath the surface.

Kennedy leapt onto the experimental theater scene of the 1960s with *Funnyhouse*, a dramatic poem of torment that confounded the daily reviewers (one major New York paper called it "a disaster, not even worthy of consideration"), but bowled over the epicures of the nascent off-Broadway movement (it won an Obie Award). Ever since, Kennedy's work has met the same extreme responses: mainstream critics and producers dismiss her plays without even taking much note, while those on the margins (myself happily among them) champion her work as revelatory, ground-breaking, and downright beautiful. Thus, while a Kennedy play may show up on the syllabus of a college course on plays by women (recently, *A Movie Star Has to Star in Black and White* was added to the *Norton Anthology of American Literature*), they tend to stay safely within the academy, as if someone has decreed that it's okay to *read* these radical, hallucinatory works, but actually to *produce* them—well, that would be going a little too far. *Funnyhouse*, or for that matter, any number of Kennedy's plays, ought to be a staple of our resident theaters, playing to audiences from Maine to California, with the regularity of works by such writers as Sam Shepard, Maria Irene Fornes, and August Wilson.

Granted, Kennedy's plays may not seem easy to put up. How exactly do you realize a stage direction like this one from *Funnyhouse*: "Jesus is a hunchback, yellow-skinned dwarf, dressed in white rags and sandals. Patrice Lumumba is a black man. His head appears to be split in two with blood and tissue in eyes"; or this one from *The Owl Answers*: " . . . Altar burning, White Bird laughs from the Dome. She who is Clara Passmore who is the Virgin Mary who is Bastard who is the Owl suddenly looks like an owl . . . "? And producers may argue that the plays are too short for an audience that demands its money's worth in terms measured by the length of their entertainment.

Of course such objections say more about the imaginative and commercial limits of our resident theaters than about the challenges of Kennedy's plays. Yet as much as these excuses reveal certain bankruptcies in the American theater scene, the issue runs deeper. First, despite thirty years of off-off-Broadway, American directors and actors — much less African-American directors and actors — have had little opportunity to work on experimental plays and as a result, are ill-prepared for the dissenting demands of Kennedy's complex style.

What is more, Kennedy suffers a fate common to most women or African-American writers: if their plays do not conform to conventional expectations of what "minority" playwrights do, they are passed over for more palatable and categorizable fare. Even today, only a smattering of plays produced in major American theaters are written by women, and those tend to remain within strict thematic and stylistic bounds. There is no place, in these institutions as they are currently constituted, for the graphic, gory depictions of rape, incest, and sexual violence that are at the core of Kennedy's early plays, little room for the flights of one of America's grandest imaginations.

As a black writer, Kennedy falls outside of what is acceptable as well, which means that she avoids being pigeonholed as a "political" writer (great bugaboo of post-McCarthyite American theater) — but also that she is less likely to be produced. Even in 1964, with the premiere of *Funnyhouse*, director Michael Kahn had to explain to people that this was not a " 'can-I-live-in-your-neighborhood' kind of play." Other experimental African-American writers who address political themes have similarly struggled to point out that they are not writing what George C. Wolfe has satirized in *The Colored Museum* as the "mama-on-the-couch play," or what Suzan-Lori Parks calls the " 'I'm-gonna-get-you-whitey' plays of the 1970s." Such disclaimers indicate the extent to which black playwrights in the United States are commonly assumed to be writing didactic, militant message plays about race.

During the 1960s and 1970s, many within the activist African-American community insisted that was what their playwrights *should* have been writing. In those years, Kennedy was criticized by activists for not working enough in the movement (she was raising two children on her own) and for being "an irrelevant black writer." They objected to her characters, who were confused about their identity and place in the world, and who did not proclaim an uncomplicated pride in being black.

In *Funnyhouse*, for instance, the protagonist Sarah rages against her blackness. Alone in her room, Sarah smacks violently against fantastical visions of historical figures. Queen Victoria, the Duchess of Hapsburg, Patrice Lumumba, and Jesus all appear, contesting Sarah's attraction to white culture, insistently reflecting the blackness she would deny, even mocking her self-loathing. The room is like a spooky hall of mirrors that twists Sarah's carefully constructed sense of self, and exposes her to herself. Like the works that followed, this play bitterly and beautifully investigates what W. E. B. Du Bois called the double consciousness of African-American life, a life that must reconcile the yoked forces of European and African experience, while refusing their synthesis.

Kennedy was nervous about the premiere of *Funnyhouse*, which had been recommended for production by Edward Albee, whose playwriting workshop she had been attending at Circle in the Square. She edited the play, removing references she thought might offend people, such as the word "nigger." But Albee interceded, telling Kennedy that the playwright must not be afraid to show her "guts" on stage.

Despite misgivings from movement activists about the play's failure to present positive role models, it deals directly, as Kennedy told the *New York Daily News* when it opened, "with being a Negro and with being any person who must learn to live." And given what the particular person in her play must learn to live *with*, it is a powerful portrait of the wreckage wrought by racism in our culture. Today, perhaps, its force is all the more palpable—and all the more horrifying—because there is less of a social movement providing a resonant context. Indeed, *Funnyhouse* stands up after nearly three decades far more solidly than, say, LeRoi Jones's *The Dutchman*—which won the *best* play Obie the year *Funnyhouse* won its award.

In sum, what most makes Kennedy's plays scare off theater producers and their narrow expectations is exactly what makes the plays so exciting: their looping, lilting language and their fuguelike, fragmented form. Kennedy's style is a kind of engaged expressionism, a poetic theater of images that is firmly rooted in the politics of race and gender. Character is frequently split in Kennedy's work, her protagonists projected through myriad personae— centuries-old royalty, contemporary revolutionaries, Hollywood movie stars, even owls and rats. Dialogue takes place not through the conversational exchange of characters addressing each other, but through the fluid interplay of visual and verbal imagery. And plot, in its conventional sense, does not even exist.

Suspense does not drive these plays; they are not focused on the question of what will happen next. Rather than following the patterns of a teleological drama, in which events lead to a climax, whose explanation is the substance of most naturalistic plays, Kennedy lets meanings emerge through the accretion of intense images over a constantly shifting ground. There are no stories that develop in linear fashion, though plot lines are sometimes parceled out in bits pieced from past, present, and future. Time itself is not linear in Kennedy's whirligig world. Thus Sister Rat can be present on stage in *A Rat's Mass*, with her rotund rodent's belly, while she and Brother Rat, in their religious recitation, assert that she is "now" in the state hospital. A procession of Jesus, Joseph, Mary, Two Wise Men, and a Shepherd can march across the theater, and provoke Brother and Sister Rat's screams, "The Nazis! The

Nazis have invaded our house." Or in *The Owl Answers*, the character called She who is Clara Passmore who is the Virgin Mary who is the Bastard who is the Owl—and who is also identified as the daughter of "the Richest White Man in the Town and somebody that cooked for him"— can be simultaneously imprisoned in the Tower of London, hurtling along in a New York subway train, and sitting in a Harlem hotel room.

With these nightmarish journeys, Kennedy fashions a new kind of narrative structure. With a black female protagonist at its center, it reinvents, as it deconstructs, the narrative structures of white, male-dominated culture: Victorian novels, Hollywood movies, Catholic rituals. If in the early plays, Kennedy's protagonists were hallucinators whose tortured psychosexual lives were being blasted open into a raw, relentless vision, in *The Alexander Plays*, the protagonist has stopped dreaming openly and started recounting. Yet while Suzanne Alexander becomes the literal narrator of her story, explaining events in straightforward first-person monologues, these works still share the early plays' suspicion of linear narrative. Contesting the interior boundaries of conventional narrative structure, Kennedy raises new questions about form and character and their theatrical relationships.

Both *The Ohio State Murders* and *She Talks to Beethoven* contain lines that could serve as evocative descriptions of Kennedy's early plays, and that offer some clues about the tacit complexities of these new works: In the first, Hampshire lectures on Hardy's *Tess of the D'Urbervilles*, stating that "Hardy absorbs Tess's personal situation into a vast system of causation"; in the second, the voice of David, broadcast by radio, quotes Frantz

Fanon discovering, "I was only an object among other objects . . . I burst apart. Now the fragments have been put together by another self." To this day, Kennedy's plays lay bare the vast system of causation, the orbit of opposing and colliding forces that shape individuals; and in her imagistic theater, those individuals are set out as objects among other objects, bursting apart, and being assembled anew.

More important for the new plays, these quotes are multiply mediated. In *The Alexander Plays* it may look as if Suzanne is relating events in the simplest way imaginable—that is, just telling what happened. But these pieces offer so many different means of giving voice to stories, and so many means of accounting for memory, that the very project of assembling recollections and shaping them into a coherent, consumable form becomes suspect— and just telling a story becomes impossible. Monologues, diaries, radio accounts, lectures, letters, poems, movie scripts (themselves mere transcriptions)—all these means of capturing and expressing experience are juxtaposed into a vast system of narrative options. And sometimes, they do not concur.

By any conventional definition, these plays are not at all dramatic. Events are described more often than depicted (in *She Talks to Beethoven* Kennedy actually asks an audience to sit and listen to a voice coming from a radio), and there is very little actual dialogue (the only person Suzanne converses with in *She Talks to Beethoven* cannot even hear). But of course that is because the action of these plays is made up not of the events of Suzanne's life but of the process of turning memory into meaning.

Kennedy creates a tangible, discomfitting tension between the ostensible story building in these plays, and their simultaneous deconstruction. One way she does this is, once again, by splitting her characters. But instead of dividing them into myriad stage personae, she cleaves them with the sharpness of time. Past and future are visited upon one another in Suzanne's stage presence; it is as if she is always speaking in the future perfect.

At the same time, the violence in these plays is more muted than in earlier works, and therefore, paradoxically more ominous. In place of the stabbings and hangings of the 1970s plays, here we have unstaged murders and surmised kidnappings, descriptions of Dracula, and a bleeding scalp. Such images haunt Suzanne with a familiar persistence; if they are less aggressive than the demons pursuing Sarah and Clara and Sister Rat, it is only because they have been at it longer.

In past plays, Kennedy's young protagonists faced moments of trauma — and died of them — in dizzying, disturbing spectacles; now, Suzanne, who is older, persists beyond those traumas. She is Sarah in middle age, without a noose, Sister Rat at, say, age forty, spared the firing squad.

Surviving beyond such crises, Kennedy's characters must assimilate the unacceptable, make sense of the unintelligible. And more than ever, they "must learn how to live."

THE
Alexander
Plays

She Talks to Beethoven

First produced by River Arts in Woodstock, New York, and directed by Clinton Turner Davis in June 1989.

CHARACTERS
    LUDWIG VAN BEETHOVEN
    SUZANNE ALEXANDER A Writer

AUTHOR'S NOTE:

The music in the piece should equal in length the text.
Anonymous diary entries are from actual sources.

Scene: Accra, Ghana, in 1961, soon after independence.
   It is early evening.

*Interior of a bedroom at house on the campus at Legon, a
shuttered room, a ceiling fan, a bed covered with mosquito
netting, a shelf of books over a small writing table, and a
delicate blue phonograph. All windows except one are
shuttered. That window overlooks a winding road. The
side of the room that is shuttered is dim.* SUZANNE ALEX-
ANDER *listens to a small radio. She is American, black, a*

pretty woman in her thirties. Part of her arm and shoulder are wrapped or bandaged in gauze. Placed on a shelf opposite her bed are a group of x-ray slides, the kind doctors use to analyze a patient's illness. She studies them, watches the road, and listlessly writes a line or so in a notebook. On the shelf is a photograph of Kwame Nkrumah, a book on Ludwig van Beethoven, a wedding photo of SUZANNE *and her husband, David, and a mural displaying various scenes of Ghana's' independence.* SUZANNE *is dressed in a robe of kinte cloth.*

From outside Ghanaians play stringed musical instruments as they walk in an evening procession.

SUZANNE: *(Reads over notes from published diaries.)* "The production of *Fidelio* was anticipated by months of increasing tension as the war with Napoleon escalated. Soldiers were quartered in all suburbs. At nine o'clock houses were locked and all inns cleared out. At Ulm on 20 October the Russians conceded defeat to the French. Ten days later, Bernadotte and the French army entered Salzburg. One saw baggage and travel-carriages passing. In the afternoon I went with Therese to the Danube. We saw the possessions of the Court being shipped off. The Court is sending everything away, even bedwarmers and shoetrees. It looks as if they have no intention of ever coming back to Vienna.

After lunch Eppinger came with the devastating

news that the Russians have retreated as far as Saint Polten. Vienna is in great danger of being swept over by marauding Chasseurs."

(Suzanne *suddenly turns to the radio.*)

Voice on Radio: I came into this world with the desire to give order to things: my one great hope was to be of the world and I discovered I was only an object among other objects. Sealed into that crushing objecthood I turned beseechingly to others. Their attention was a liberation endowing me once more with an agility that I had thought lost. But just as I reached the other side I stumbled and the movements, the attitudes, the glances of the others fixed me there. I burst apart. Now the fragments have been put together by another self.

Another Voice on the Radio: And that was David Alexander, the American professor of African poetry, here at the University . . . reading from Frantz Fanon. Mr. Alexander is still missing. Alexander traveled with Fanon in Blida. His wife, also American, the writer Suzanne Alexander, is recovering from an unspecified illness. It is known that she was writing a play about Ludwig van Beethoven when she was stricken. Alexander was by her side at the hospital when he suddenly vanished two nights ago. Mrs. Alexander has returned to their home on the campus at Legon near Accra.

(*Musical passage of African stringed instruments.*)

SUZANNE: *(Reading from published diaries.)* "The final rehearsal was on 22 May but the promised new overture was still in the pen of the creator. The orchestra was called to rehearsal in the morning of the performance. Beethoven did not come. After waiting a long time we drove to his lodgings to bring him but he lay in bed sleeping soundly. Beside him stood a goblet with wine and a biscuit in it. The sheets of the overture were scattered on the floor and bed. A burnt out candle showed he had worked far into the night."

(The room appears out of the darkness. SUZANNE *rises and crosses to* BEETHOVEN *and stands staring at him.)*

RADIO: Although the couple are American they have lived in West Africa for a number of years and together started a newspaper that was a forerunner to *Black Orpheus* bringing together poems, stories, and novels by African writers as well as Afro-Americans, some in exile in England. It is known that often Alexander jests with his wife about her continued deep love for European artists such as Sibelius, Chopin, and Beethoven and indeed if anyone in Accra wants to hear these composers one has only to pass the windows of the delightful white stucco house among the fragrant flowers on the campus at Legon.

*(*SUZANNE *stares at* BEETHOVEN*)*

SUZANNE: *(Reading published notes from the diary of _____.)* "Beethoven was the most celebrated of the living composers living in Vienna. The neglect of his person which he exhibited gave him a somewhat wild appearance. His features were strong and prominent; his eye was full of rude energy; his hair, which neither comb nor scissors seemed to have visited for years, overshadowed his broad brow in a quantity and confusion to which only the snakes round a Gorgon's head offer a parallel."

You worked into the night.

BEETHOVEN: Yes. Tonight is the opening of *Fidelio*.

SUZANNE: Did I awaken you?

BEETHOVEN: I was dreaming of my mother and how every year on Saint Magdalen's day, her name and birthdate, we would celebrate. The music stands would be brought out. And chairs would be placed everywhere and a canopy set up in the room where the portrait of my grandfather hung. We decorated the canopy with flowers, laurel branches, and foliage. Early in the evening my mother retired. And by ten o'clock everyone would be ready. The tuning up would begin and my mother would be awakened. She would then dress and be led in and seated in a beautifully decorated chair under the canopy. At that very moment magnificent music would strike up resounding throughout the neighborhood. And when the music ended, a meal was served and company ate and drank and danced until the celebration came to an end.

(Loud voices from outside.)

BEETHOVEN: That must be the directors of the theater for the new overture. It's not finished.

(BEETHOVEN *starts toward the door and vanishes.*)

SUZANNE: Wait. I want to talk to you. Before David disappeared he questioned me on passages I wrote about you in Vienna. We argued.

(*She looks at drawings* BEETHOVEN *has in his room and sheet music on the floor. Suddenly she runs back to the open window watching the road for her husband. A long passage of the African stringed music from the procession on the road.* BEETHOVEN *returns and sits at the piano composing. He seems to have forgotten* SUZANNE. *She continues looking out of the window, listening to the African stringed music, watching the road for her husband, David. The music now changes into the overture* BEETHOVEN *is composing.*)

RADIO: Has Alexander been murdered?
SUZANNE: I've been unable to work. David helps me with all the scenes about you.
BEETHOVEN: Perhaps you might seek a retreat in the woods, Suzanne. It makes me happy to wander among herbs and trees.

(*He continues composing music.*)

SUZANNE: Tell me about your summers in Vienna . . . I have

read life in Vienna during the hot months was not pleasant.

BEETHOVEN: Yes, like tonight here in Accra it was not pleasant. There were over a thousand horse-drawn cabs and over three hundred coaches of hire traveling across granite cobbles. They raised a terrible dust which hovered in the air the whole summer and even during part of the winter. It was like a dirty fog. I went to Baden and worked on a symphony.

SUZANNE: And your fame? I must ask you, are you happy with your fame?

BEETHOVEN: I do not like or have anything to do with people who refused to believe in me when I had not yet achieved fame. My three string quartets were all finished before fame came.

(He composes. She returns to the window. He composes music.)

SUZANNE: *(From diary of _____.)* "While he was working, he would stand at the washbasin and pour great pitchersful of water over his hands, at the same time howling the whole gamut of the scale, ascending and descending; then pace the room, his eyes fixed in a stare, jot down a few notes and again return to his water pouring and howling."

(Music from Fidelio*)*

BEETHOVEN: You've argued about me?

SUZANNE: Yes. David says many scenes of you are too

10

romantic—and that I must read more diaries about you. He gave me one by a Baron about this very room.

SUZANNE: *(Reads to* BEETHOVEN.*)* "I wended my way to the unapproachable composer's home, and at the door it struck me that I had chosen the day ill, for, having to make an official visit thereafter, I was wearing the everyday habiliments of the Council of State. To make matters worse, his lodging was next to the city wall, and as Napoleon had ordered its destruction, blasts had just been set off under his windows."

RADIO: Has David Alexander been murdered? The outspoken professor at the University of Legon is still missing. As we have reported, Alexander worked with Fanon in Blida and was friends with the late Patrice Lumumba. Now that Fanon may be dying of cancer, Alexander has become highly vocal in keeping Fanon's words alive. We've played you his rendering of Fanon's essays and now we listen to David Alexander's poetry. It has never been clear, Alexander has said on many occasions, who the enemies of Fanon are and even though Ghana has won its independence, as Osegefo also continues to remind us: there are still enemies. Alexander was hated by many for his writing on the clinics and Fanon, and for his statements on the mental condition of the colonized patients. At first it was thought that when Alexander disappeared he was writing about one of the patients at the hospital at Legon, but now it has been revealed he was there waiting to hear the results of his wife's undisclosed surgery. And was indeed by her bedside and disappeared while she slept after surgery.

The Alexanders, an inseparable couple, often read their works together and have written a series of poems and essays jointly. It has been learned that at the hospital while sitting at his wife's side Alexander made sketches of his wife's illness and explained the progress and surgery procedures to her.

(Music. Passage that BEETHOVEN *is composing.)*

(From outside voices are heard shouting "Karl, Karl, Karl!" BEETHOVEN *rushes from the room.* SUZANNE *stands at the window. Music from the road blends with voices shouting, "Karl!"* BEETHOVEN *enters.)*

BEETHOVEN: My nephew Karl has tried to shoot himself. He's wounded. He's been taken to his mother's house.

SUZANNE: We'll go there.

BEETHOVEN: No. I can't. He told the police he was tormented by me and that is why he tried to kill himself and he does not want to see me. He says he's miserable and he's grown worse because I want him to live his life according to my expectation of him.

SUZANNE: *(Writes in her manuscript.)* Beethoven's nephew Karl tried to shoot himself. The tension between the two had reached a crisis. The incident left Beethoven in a shocked state. He was the only person Beethoven really loved to the point of idolatry.

RADIO: And again . . . Alexander . . . reading Fanon . . . still missing . . . where . . . has he been murdered?

SUZANNE: We could still walk to Karl's house near the Danube and look into his window. Perhaps you can call to him.

(Light in room fades. Now they are walking near the Danube. They look up at what could be Karl's windows.)

BEETHOVEN: *(Shouts.)* Karl, Karl, Karl!
BEETHOVEN calls again: Karl!

(Long silence.)

BEETHOVEN: We've come far, Suzanne. We won't get back to Dobling until nearly four now.
SUZANNE: *(Writing.)* His nephew refused to see him. We did not get back to Dobling where Beethoven lived until seven. As we walked he started humming, sometimes howling, singing indefinite notes. "A theme for the last part of the overture has occurred to me," he said.

(Room appears again. BEETHOVEN enters, running to the pianoforte. Music.)

RADIO: *(David's voice reads an excerpt from Fanon.)* Yesterday awakening to the world I saw the sky utterly and wholly. I wanted to rise but fell paralyzed. Without responsibility, nothingness, and infinitely I began to weep.

(Music. BEETHOVEN composes.)

SUZANNE: *(Reads from the diary of _____.)* "Beethoven misunderstood me very often, and had to use the utmost concentration when I was speaking, to get my meaning. That, of course, embarrassed and disturbed me very much. It disturbed him, too, and this led him to speak more himself and very loudly. He told me a lot about his life and about Vienna. He was venomous and embittered. He raged about everything, and was dissatisfied with everything. He cursed Austria and Vienna in particular. He spoke quickly and with great vivacity. He often banged his fist on the piano and made such a noise that it echoed around the room."

(SUZANNE writes while talking to BEETHOVEN.)

SUZANNE: You must dress now for the concert.

BEETHOVEN: Please go to the theater with me.

SUZANNE: I must watch the road for David.

BEETHOVEN: We'll stay together until David arrives. We'll watch the road and go to the theater together.

RADIO: An hour ago there was an accident near Kumasi that seemed to have some connection to Alexander but now that has been discounted.

RADIO: It is now believed that David Alexander, learning of a plot against his life while he sat at his wife's bedside, chose to vanish to protect her, his colleague and fellow writer. Professor Alexander still continues to speak about attaining true independence. So now it is believed he is alive and waiting for the time when he can return home. Included in the next selection are two poems read by the couple together from their recording. The first selection is by Diop.

(Radio fades.)

BEETHOVEN: Is it true that David made drawings of your surgery as he sat by your side so that you would not be frightened?

SUZANNE: Yes.

BEETHOVEN: How very romantic. And do you believe that he vanished to protect you?

SUZANNE: Yes.

BEETHOVEN: And you compose poems and read together?

SUZANNE: Yes.

BEETHOVEN: What scenes did you fight over?

SUZANNE: He wanted a scene where you read your contracts, a scene where you talk about money.

(BEETHOVEN *laughs.*)

BEETHOVEN: Do you disagree a great deal about your work together?

SUZANNE: No, only over this play. We set out to write it together years ago, then it became mine. Even on the morning of the surgery we argued about it.

(BEETHOVEN *laughs.*)

BEETHOVEN: I feel David will return by morning, perhaps on the road with the musicians, perhaps even in disguise.

SUZANNE: Disguise.

BEETHOVEN: Yes.

RADIO: A body has been found in a swamp in Abijan. Is it Alexander? Has he been murdered?

(SUZANNE *begins to unwrap her bandages.*)

BEETHOVEN: Why do you unwrap the gauze?

SUZANNE: The bandage is wrapped on my wound. I'm to unwrap it tonight and if the wound is pale white I'm still sick.

(BEETHOVEN *starts to help her slowly unwrap the gauze. She does not look at her surgical wound as he unwraps the gauze.*)

SUZANNE: What color?

BEETHOVEN: The color is pale white.

(*Silence.*)

BEETHOVEN: How long have you been sick?

SUZANNE: Two and one half years?

BEETHOVEN: You mustn't worry. I've foreseen my death many times. It will be in winter. In Vienna. My friends will come from Graz. (*He embraces her.*)

(SUZANNE *sits at* BEETHOVEN'*s piano. He walks to the window.*)

Suzanne: *(Reads from the diary of _____.)* "Before Beethoven's death I found him greatly disturbed and jaundiced all over his body. A frightful choleric attack had threatened his life the preceding night. Trembling and shivering he bent double because of the pains which raged in his liver and intestines; and his feet, hitherto moderately inflamed, were tremendously swollen. From this time on dropsy developed, the liver showed plain indication of hard nodules, there was an increase of jaundice. The disease moved onward with gigantic strides. Already in the third week there came incidents of nocturnal suffocation."

(Radio.)

Voice on Radio: A recording of Alexander reading David Diop:

> *Listen comrades of the struggling centuries*
> *To the keen clamour of the Negro from Africa*
> > *to the*
> *Americas they have killed Mamba*
> *As they killed the seven of Martinsville*
> *or the Madagascan down there in the pale light*
> > *of*
> *the prisons. . . .*

(Room fades. They are backstage. BEETHOVEN *is dressed formally for the theater. Music from stage. Orchestra rehearsing* Fidelio. *They both watch the road.)*

SUZANNE: You must be happy tonight about *Fidelio.*

(He does not speak.)

BEETHOVEN: Suzanne, because of your anguish I want to share a secret with you. For the last six years I have been afflicted with an incurable complaint. From year to year my hopes of being cured have gradually been shattered and finally I have been forced to accept the prospect of permanent infirmity. I am obliged to live in solitude. If I try to ignore my infirmity I am cruelly reminded of it. Yet I cannot bring myself to say to people, "Speak up, shout, for I am deaf."

(Music from stage, orchestra rehearsing Fidelio.*)*

In the theater I have to place myself quite close to the orchestra in order to understand what the actor is saying, and at a distance I cannot hear the high notes of instruments or voices. As for the spoken voice it is surprising that some people have never noticed my deafness; but since I have always been liable to fits of absentmindedness, they attribute my hardness of hearing to that. Sometimes, too, I can scarcely hear a person who speaks softly; I can hear sounds, it is true, but cannot make out the words. But if anyone shouts,

I can't bear it. I beg you not to say anything about my condition to anyone. I am only telling you this as a secret. Suzanne, if my trouble persists may I visit you next spring?

SUZANNE: I had no idea you were going deaf.

BEETHOVEN: Yes, in fact you must write any further questions in this little conversation book. I've been trying to hide them from you. *(He gives her the conversation books.)*

BEETHOVEN: You must write what you want to say to me in them. I cannot hear you.

SUZANNE: Ludwig! *(She embraces him.)*

RADIO: *(SUZANNE's voice reads from Fanon.)* At the level of individuals violence is a cleansing force, it frees a man from despair and inaction.

RADIO: It has been learned that the group who plotted to kill David Alexander has been discovered near Kumasi and has been arrested. It is safe for Alexander to return to Accra. And it is reported that Nkrumah himself met with the revolutionary poet a few hours ago and reported to him the details of his would-be assassins' capture.

SUZANNE: *(Suddenly.)* Ludwig, why is David's handwriting in your conversation books? This poem is in David's own handwriting.

(BEETHOVEN *does not answer.*)

(SUZANNE *studies the conversation books.*)

SUZANNE: Ludwig! There is a message from David, a love

poem of Senghor's. Whenever David wants to send me a message he puts a poem inside my papers, in a book he knows I will read.

(She writes in conversation book and reads.)

SUZANNE: Be not astonished, my love, if at times my song grows dark
If I change my melodious reed for the khalam and the tama's beat
And the green smell of the rice fields for galloping rumble of the tabalas.
Listen to the threats of old sorcerers, to the thundering wrath of God!
Ah, maybe tomorrow the purple voice of your song-maker will be silent forever.
That's why today my song is so urgent and my fingers bleed on my khalam.

(She opens another conversation book. Music from the stage.)

SUZANNE: *(Reads David's words.)* Suzanne, please continue writing scenes. Please continue writing scenes we talked about.

(Lights fade backstage and come up on concert hall. BEE-THOVEN now stands before the orchestra, stage center. He waves baton wildly. It is obvious he does not hear. Music stops. He starts again. He waves wildly, throwing the singers and orchestra off beat and into confusion. Silence. He

20

calls SUZANNE *to his side. She writes in the book.* BEETHOVEN *buries his face and rushes to the wings leaving the orchestra.* SUZANNE *writes.)*

SUZANNE: Ludwig was still desperately trying to conduct in public and insisted upon conducting rehearsals even though by now during the concert the orchestra knew to ignore his beat and to follow instead the Kapellmeister who stood behind him.

(BEETHOVEN *returns stage center. As she speaks* BEETHOVEN *conducts. Music.)*

SUZANNE: At *Fidelio* Ludwig waved his baton back and forth with violent motions, not hearing a note. If he thought it should be piano he crouched down almost under the podium and if he wanted faster he jumped up with strange gestures uttering strange sounds. Yet the evening was a triumph.

(SUZANNE *stands at window writing. A shadow appears on the road.)*

SUZANNE: David!

(The deaf BEETHOVEN *turns to her, smiles, conducting violently. Music.)*

SUZANNE: *(Reads from the diary of _____.)* "As for the musical success of this memorable evening, it could be favorably compared to any event ever presented in that venerable theatre. Alas, the man to whom all this honor was addressed could hear none of it, for when at the end of the performance the audience broke into enthusiastic applause, he remained standing with his back to them. Then the contralto soloist had the presence of mind to turn the master toward the proscenium and show him the cheering throng throwing their hats into the air and waving their handkerchiefs. He acknowledged his gratitude with a bow. This set off an almost unprecedented volley of jubilant applause that went on and on as the joyful listeners sought to express their thanks for the pleasure they had just been granted."

(Concert scene fades to BEETHOVEN*'s room.* SUZANNE *stands in the center staring at* BEETHOVEN*'s grand piano, his chair, manuscript paper.)*

SUZANNE: *(Reads from the diary of _____.)* "Monday, the 26th of March 1827 was a freezing day. From Silesia and the Sudeten peaks, a north wind blew across the Wienerwald. Everywhere the ground lay under a soft blanket of fresh, silent snow. The long winter had been raw, damp, cold, and frosty; on that day it showed no sign of releasing its grip on the land.

By four o'clock the lights of Vienna, the street lamps, the candles of myriad rooms, began to pierce the overcast gloom. On the second floor of the Schwarzspanierhaus, the House of the Black Spaniard, to the west of the old city walls, lay a man who had all but run his course. In a large, sparsely furnished room of 'sad appearance,' amid squalor and books and manuscript paper and within sight of his prized mahogany Broadwood grand, Beethoven lost hold of life. On a roughly made bed, unconscious, he was at that moment as broken and finished as his piano. The elements continued to rage. Flurries of snow drifted against the window. Then, 'there was suddenly a loud clap of thunder accompanied by a bolt of lightning . . . Beethoven opened his eyes, raised his right hand, and, his fist clenched, looked upward for several seconds . . . As he let his hand sink down onto the bed again, his eyes half closed . . . There was no more breathing, no more heartbeat! The great composer's spirit fled from this world."

So remembered Anselm Huttenbrenner, who recorded Beethoven's end even more poignantly in the terseness of a diary entry: "Ludwig van Beethoven's death, in the evening, toward six o'clock of dropsy in his fifty-seventh year. He is no longer!"

(She cries. Music from the road, of African stringed instruments. Suzanne *rushes to the door.)*

Suzanne: David. You sent Beethoven until you returned. Didn't you?

David's Voice: *(Not unlike* Beethoven*'s.)* I knew he would console you while I was absent.

END

The Ohio State Murders

The Ohio State Murders was commissioned by the Great Lakes
Theater Festival (Gerald Freedman, artistic director; Mary Bill,
managing director) through a grant from the New Works Program
of the Ohio Arts Council. The play received its world premiere at
the Great Lakes Theater Festival on March 7, 1992, with the following cast:

Suzanne Alexander	RUBY DEE
Suzanne	BELLARY DARDEN
David Alexander	MICHAEL EARLY
Robert Hampshire	ALLAN BYRNE
Aunt Louise	IRMA HALL
Val	RICK WILLIAMS
Iris Ann	LESLIE HOLLAND
Suzanne's Father	MICHAEL EARLY

Directed by GERALD FREEDMAN; set design conceived by GERALD
FREEDMAN and executed by JOHN EZELL; projections by KURT SHARP
and JESSE EPSTEIN; costumes coordinated by AL KOHOUT; lighting de-
signed by CYNTHIA STILLINGS; sound design by STANLEY J. M. KOZAK

CHARACTERS

SUZANNE ALEXANDER (1949-1952) The young writer as
a student attending Ohio State from 1949 to 1950

SUZANNE ALEXANDER (Present) A well-known black
writer visiting Ohio State to give a talk on the imagery in
her work

DAVID ALEXANDER A law student she will marry

ROBERT HAMPSHIRE An English professor at Ohio State

MRS. TYLER Suzanne's landlady

VAL A friend

IRIS ANN Suzanne's roommate

MISS DAWSON Head of the dorm

TIME: *Present.*

SETTING: *Night.*

*Stacks: hundreds of books on "O" level beneath the li-
brary at Ohio State.*

A window high in the distance from which can be seen University Hall, a vast dark structure and falling snow. The snow falls throughout the play.

Sections of the stacks become places on campus during the play.

Suzanne enters the stacks, wanders, gazes at the distant window and snow. She takes out a paper, studies it, gazes about her, reads from paper rehearsing a talk.

SUZANNE (Present): I was asked to talk about the violent imagery in my work; bloodied heads, severed limbs, dead father, dead Nazis, dying Jesus. The chairman said, we do want to hear about your brief years here at Ohio State but we also want you to talk about violent imagery in your stories and plays. When I visited Ohio State last year it struck me as a series of disparate dark landscapes just as it had in 1949, the autumn of my freshman year.

   I used to write down locations in order to learn the campus: the oval, behind the green, the golf hut, behind Zoology, the tennis courts beyond the golf hut, the Olitangy River, the stadium off to the right, the main library at the head of the Oval, the old union across from the dorm, High Street at the end of the path, downtown Columbus, the Deschler Wallach, Lazarus, the train station. The geography made me anxious.

The zigzagged streets beyond the Oval were regions of Law, Medicine, Mirror Lake, the Greek theater, the lawn behind the dorm where the white girls sunned.

The ravine that would be the scene of the murder and Mrs. Tyler's boarding house in the Negro district.

The music I remembered most was a song called "Don't Go Away Mad," and the music from *A Place in the Sun*, that movie with Elizabeth Taylor and Montgomery Clift based on Theodore Dreiser's *American Tragedy*.

(SUZANNE *takes out a picture of David running the 100-yard dash at Ohio State.*

David is an extraordinarily handsome young black man. He looks like Frantz Fanon, whose biography he will one day write.)

SUZANNE (Present): This is a picture of my husband, David, who, as you know, is a writer, political activist, and biographer of Frantz Fanon. Most people don't know David started out as a lawyer.

Although we were both at Ohio State in the winter of 1950 I had not met David. But I had seen this photograph of him running the 100-yard dash at Ohio State's spring track meet.

I knew he was a state champion and now he was in law school. David had lived in the boarding house that was to become my home. Mrs. Tyler hung this picture in her hallway. She loved David Alexander. That was later.

But first I started my freshman year in the fall of '49.

I took a required English survey course although I was not an English major. I had declared no major course of study. We read Thomas Hardy.

SCENE: *Quonset hut.* HAMPSHIRE *enters.* SUZANNE (1949) *watches him. As a student she wears pale skirt, sweater (powder blue), saddle shoes, and socks.*

SUZANNE (Present): The professor was a young man. His name was Hampshire. He was small and dressed rather formally in a tweed suit with a vest. He always walked straight to the lectern and without any introduction started his lectures.

(HAMPSHIRE *looks at his notes.* SUZANNE [1949] *watches him intently. She is fragile, pale.*)

The class was held in a quonset hut, a temporary barrack-like structure that had room for fifty to sixty students. These huts were built to house the overflow of students after the war. Professor Hampshire read from *Tess of the D'Urbervilles.*

HAMPSHIRE: "In spite of the unpleasant initiation of the day before, Tess inclined to the freedom and novelty of her new position in the morning when the sun shone, now that she was once installed there; and she was curious to test her powers in the unexpected direction asked of her, so as to ascertain her chance of retaining her post.

As soon as she was alone within the walled garden she sat herself down on a coop, and seriously screwed up her mouth for the long-neglected practice. She found her former ability to have degenerated to the production of a hollow rush of wind through the lips and no clear note at all."

(HAMPSHIRE *draws a map.*)

SUZANNE: On a makeshift blackboard he drew a map of Wessex.
HAMPSHIRE: Blackmore Vale, Marlott, Edgdon Heath, New Forest, Chalk Newton, Casterbridge.

(SUZANNE *continues to watch him intently.*)

SCENE ENDS.

SUZANNE (Present): *(Stands in stacks.)* These places in Wessex, Marlott, New Forest, Chalk Newton intrigued me as did *Tess of the D'Urbervilles.*

One afternoon late, almost early evening, I walked over behind the Oval to the English Department and inquired about the catalog for English majors. A secretary said, "Come back any morning around ten. A Miss Smith will give you the information about becoming an English major. What is your major now?" she asked.

I told her I was undeclared.

I didn't know there were no "Negro" students in the English Department. It was thought that we were not able to master the program. They would allow you to take no more than two required freshman courses. After that you had to apply to the English Department to take courses that were all said to be for majors.

In my dorm across from the Old Union there were six hundred girls. Twelve of us were blacks. We occupied six places, rooming together two in a room.

The other dorms, Canfield and Neil, each also housed a few black girls.

The schools I had attended in Cleveland were an even mixture of immigrant and black. You were judged on grades. But here race was foremost.

Very few Negroes walked on High Street above the University. It wasn't that you were not allowed but you were discouraged from doing so. Above the university was a residential district encompassed by a steep ravine. I never saw this ravine until the two days I visited Bobby at his house (the ravine was where the faculty lived).

A year and a half later one of my baby twin daughters would be found dead there. That was later.

But in my freshman year the continuing happiness was Professor Hampshire's discussion of the Victorian novel.

When he lectured, his small pale face was expressionless. Only his blue eyes conveyed anger, joy, vitality.

SCENE: *Quonset hut, 1949. As* SUZANNE *watches* HAMPSHIRE *lecture she becomes excited, leaning forward listening to him more intently than ever.*

HAMPSHIRE: The idea of Chance only reminds the reader of the sphere of ideal possibilities of what ought to be happening but is not. The illusion of freedom diminishes in the course of Hardy's novels. The net narrows and finally closes.

Inherent in almost all Hardy's characters are those natural instincts which become destructive because social convention suppresses them, attempting to make the human spirit conform to the "letter."

Hardy absorbs Tess's personal situation into a vast system of causation.

SCENE ENDS.

SUZANNE (Present): For a long time no one knew who the killer was. She was the one I had called Cathi. But that was later.

Before Christmas of my freshman quarter, Professor Hampshire wrote on my paper, "Make appointment to see me."

SCENE: *English office.* SUZANNE *and* HAMPSHIRE, 1949.

SUZANNE: His office in the English Department was along a path beyond the Oval. I seldom walked there and once I left the Oval I got lost on the streets on that side of the campus and was almost late for my four o'clock appointment.

It was dark.

He was sitting in a greyish office with several empty desks.

SCENE: *English office.* SUZANNE *enters in saddle oxfords, skirt, matching sweater, cloth woolen coat. Again she wears powder blue, a popular color in 1949.*

SUZANNE (Present): I was quite nervous. It was the first time a professor at Ohio State had asked to see me.

(In the office SUZANNE *sits opposite* HAMPSHIRE.*)*

SUZANNE (Present): He was crouched over his desk writing and seemed smaller than in class, very pale, glasses, the same grayish woolen suit.

SUZANNE: *(In office.)* Professor Hampshire, you wrote on my paper you wanted to see me.

HAMPSHIRE: Oh yes, Suzanne, sit down, please. Did you bring your paper?

SUZANNE: Yes.

HAMPSHIRE: Let me see it.

SUZANNE (Present): For a moment he seemed to forget me and read the brief paper in its entirety. For a moment watching him I realized he was a man of about thirty. I later was to discover he was a lecturer and this was his first year at Ohio State.

HAMPSHIRE: What is your major?

SUZANNE: I am undeclared. But if I do well this quarter I want to apply to take another English course in the spring, but I know I have to have special permission for further English courses.

SUZANNE (Present): He didn't seem to hear me.

HAMPSHIRE: *(In his office.)* Did you write this paper yourself?

SUZANNE: Yes, Professor Hampshire.

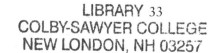

HAMPSHIRE: What reference books did you use?

SUZANNE: I used no reference books. I wrote this paper late one night in the dorm, the night before it was due.

SUZANNE (Present): He returned the paper to me, staring at the desk top. Suddenly he looked up.

HAMPSHIRE: Have you read Hardy before?

SUZANNE (Present): He didn't seem to want to continue speaking. I tried to tell him that I wanted to study more English courses, how much I loved literature. But he stood up interrupting me. He didn't speak but gathered his books together. And stared at me, then nodded. I saw the conference was over.

(SUZANNE *stands in office, moves away staring back at* HAMPSHIRE.)

OFFICE SCENE ENDS.

SCENE: *Stacks. From the window snow is falling.* SUZANNE (Present) *studies her paper.*

SUZANNE (1949) *walks across the Oval in darkness.*

SUZANNE (Present): I got lost again between two buildings behind University Hall.

Walking back in the darkness I remembered passages of my paper. And I remembered the comments Professor Hampshire had written on the margins.

SUZANNE (1949): *(Stands on Oval.)*

"Paper conveys a profound feeling for the material."

"Paper has unusual empathy for Tess."

"The language of the paper seems an extension of Hardy's own language."

(*She hears* HAMPSHIRE's *voice.*)

HAMPSHIRE: It's brilliant. It's brilliant.

SCENE ENDS.

SCENE: *Dorm. Lights on dark corridors and a dim small room lit by a single lamp.*

IRIS ANN *is lying across the bed crying. Like* SUZANNE *she wears a pale skirt and sweater (possibly pink) and like* SUZANNE *her hair is in a soft page boy.*

From the corridors we hear sounds of muffled laughing and talking.

SUZANNE *enters room.*

SUZANNE (Present): At the dorm my roommate, Iris Ann, was waiting for me to eat. Iris was lying on the bed crying. Her boyfriend had broken their engagement. We went down to the dining room and ate as usual at one of the tables where the Negro girls sat.

(Scene in dorm ends with SUZANNE *looking at* IRIS ANN.*)*

SUZANNE (Present): After dinner we walked across the wet grass up to High Street. The path wound around a new structure half finished. We chattered. All except Iris Ann. After dinner it was not uncommon for us to go to Tomaine Tommy's and bring back cheeseburgers to be eaten later that night. On the way back to the dorm Iris started sobbing. It had begun to snow.

35

And often music came from the corridors. A song called "Don't Go Away Mad" was popular.

(Sound of music in the corridors.)

SUZANNE (Present): In class the next week Professor Hampshire read again from Hardy.

SCENE: *Quonset hut.* SUZANNE *stares up at* HAMPSHIRE.

HAMPSHIRE: *(Reads.)* " . . . It was not until she was quite close that he could believe her to be Tess.

'I saw you — turn away from the station — just before I got there — and I have been following you all this way!'

She was so pale, so breathless, so quivering in every muscle, that he did not ask her a single question, but seizing her hand, and pulling it within his arm, he led her along. To avoid meeting any possible wayfarers he left the high road, and took a footpath under some fir trees. When they were deep among the moaning boughs he stopped and looked at her inquiringly.

'Angel,' she said, as if waiting for this, 'Do you know what I have been running after you for? To tell you that I have killed him!' A pitiful white smile lit her face as she spoke.

'What!' said he, thinking from the strangeness of her manner that she was in some delirium.

'I have done it — I don't know how,' she continued. 'Still, I owed it to you, and to myself Angel. I feared long ago, when I struck him on the mouth with my glove, that I might do it some day for the trap he set for me in my simple youth, and his wrong to you through me. He has come between us and ruined us, and now he can never do it any more. I never loved him at all, Angel, as I loved you. You know it, don't you? You believe it? You didn't come back to me, and I was obliged to go back to him. Why did you go away—why did you—when I loved you so? I can't think why you did it. But I don't blame you; only, Angel, will you forgive me my sin against you, now I have killed him? I thought as I ran along that you would be sure to forgive me now I have done that. It came to me as a shining light that I should get you back that way. I could not bear the loss of you any longer—you don't know how entirely I was unable to bear your not loving me! Say you do now, dear, dear husband; say you do, now I have killed him!'

'I do love you, Tess—O, I do—it is all come back!' he said, tightening his arms round her with fervid pressure. 'But how do you mean—you have killed him?'

'I mean that I have,' she murmured in a reverie.

'What, bodily? Is he dead?'

'Yes. He heard me crying about you, and he bitterly taunted me; and called you by a foul name; and then I did it. My heart could not bear it.' "

(SUZANNE *cries.*

HAMPSHIRE *glances at her.*
He leaves quonset hut.
She remains in her seat.)

(Dorm music.)

SUZANNE (Present): One by one the white girls went to live on The Row. Their pattern was to live in the dorm their freshman year and then go live in The House. Although we had sororities, Alpha Kappa Alpha and Delta Sigma Theta, we did not have "houses." We met in rooms on campus or in private homes. So we remained in the dorm.

(Dorm music. SUZANNE [1950] *sitting in dorm room.)*

SUZANNE: Sorority Row right off High Street seemed a city in itself: the cluster of streets with the columned mansions sitting on top of the lawn appeared like a citadel.

SUZANNE: *(Reads her book of symbols.)* "A city should have a sacred geography never arbitrary but planned in strict accord with the dictates of a doctrine that the society upholds."

SCENE ENDS.

SUZANNE (Present): I never walked on those blocks and saw them only from Mrs. Tyler's coupe. There was no reason for Negroes to walk in those blocks.

SCENE: *University Hall, 1950.* IRIS ANN *and* SUZANNE *watch vivid footage of film* Potemkin.

SUZANNE (Present): Before she dropped out of Ohio State, Iris Ann wanted to be a music major. She had been first violinist in her high school orchestra. She told me some of the music students went to University Hall to a film society. We went a few times, walking across the Oval in the rain and saw a movie called *The Battleship Potemkin*. The movie was shown on the ground level of the hall. Down the massive stairwells with iron flowered balustrades we walked to a small auditorium.

I had never seen a movie as old as that. There were two showings. We went back to see the other half.

SUZANNE: (At *Potemkin*.) Who is Eisenstein?

SUZANNE (Present): Iris Ann said she would ask one of the music students, Sonia. Sonia gave Iris Ann a typed paragraph on a small piece of paper describing the movie.

(SUZANNE [1950] *and* IRIS ANN *continue watching* Potemkin.)

SUZANNE (Present): *(Reads paper.)* "*Battleship Potemkin* concentrates on the mutiny on a battleship of the Black Sea Fleet during the 1905 Revolution with the massacre on the Odessa steps. Down a seemingly endless flight of steps march soldiers advancing on the fleeing citizens."

SUZANNE (Present): There was more on the scenes I had been drawn to.

(SUZANNE *and* IRIS ANN *continue watching film.*)

SUZANNE (Present): *(Reads paper.)* "The storming of the Winter Palace, the dismemberment of the Tsar's Statue and a dead horse caught at the top of an opening drawbridge."

   When we went back to see the second half I tried to remember what I had read. I asked Iris Ann were any of her music students there. She said she had seen one down front of the auditorium. I went to the library and tried to find out more about "this Eisenstein."

   For some reason the crumpled bit of paper Sonia had given Iris Ann about *Potemkin* became important to me. I kept it in the top desk drawer in my room and would unfold it and read it over.

SUZANNE: *(At* Potemkin, SUZANNE *studies film.) Battleship Potemkin* concentrates on the mutiny on a battleship of the Black Sea Fleet during the 1905 Revolution with the massacre on the Odessa Steps . . . the storming of the Winter Palace . . . the dismemberment of the Tsar's statue . . .

SCENE ENDS

SUZANNE (Present): Iris Ann could play the violin beautifully. And sometimes she'd go into the study room at the end of the corridor and practice. I asked her about the courses she was taking. They're all theory, she said. Sue, I just like to play. I've studied since I was eight at the Institute. But here courses are all theory.

She studied the theory books often on Saturday and Sunday.

Her uncle, a well-known doctor from Akron, came to visit us one Sunday. He made Iris Ann come out of the study room. That department is putting you under too much pressure, he said. I don't think they want you.

I became pregnant the following Christmas, 1950. My parents thought I spent the last day of my break with Iris in Akron but I had come back to Columbus and spent two days with Bobby above the ravine.

SCENE: *Path near quonset hut, 1950s.*

SUZANNE (Present): I had not seen him after the spring quarter ended. In fact, I did not see him until the next fall in 1950. I had applied to be an English major but had been denied. They let me take a trial course on Shaw, Wilde, Molière. I had seen Professor Hampshire on his way to the quonset hut.

SUZANNE: I am taking a trial course.

HAMPSHIRE: It's a shame.

SUZANNE (Present): The previous quarter I had taken his course on *Beowulf*. Again he had liked my papers.

HAMPSHIRE: *(On path.)* It's not necessary for you to take a trial course. It's a shame.

SCENE ENDS.

SUZANNE (Present): He hurried on.

On that same path in one year we would meet.

It was February 1951 when I told him I was pregnant. He was on the same walkway that led to the hut. Within the quonset I could see students gathering. I had not seen him since December, when I had gone to his house above the ravine.

On that cold morning I stopped him as he came toward me. I had been waiting for him as he came up the steps of University Hall and onto the Oval. The immense circle of buildings was majestic amid dark trees and snow.

I told him I was pregnant.

SCENE: *Path near quonset hut.*

SUZANNE: *(Hardly audible.)* I am pregnant.

SUZANNE (Present): He stopped an instant.

HAMPSHIRE: *(On path.)* That's not possible. We were only together twice. You surely must have other relationships. It's not possible.

SUZANNE (Present): He walked past me.

HAMPSHIRE: I don't have time to talk to you, Sue. I'm giving a talk in University Hall Thursday at eight o'clock. Wait for me afterward, perhaps we can talk.

SUZANNE (Present): He left me standing at the edge of the Oval.

SCENE ENDS.

SUZANNE (Present): I remained in the dorm until March

when I was expelled. The head of the dorm, Miss Dawson, read my diaries to the dormitory committee and decided I was unsuitable. I did not fit into campus life. And after the baby was born I would not be allowed to return to the campus.

Miss D. had gone into my room and found my poems, my Judy Garland records, my essay on loneliness and race at Ohio State and the maps I had made likening my stay here to that of Tess's life at the Vale of Blackmoor.

She called me to her office at the top of the stairs. She was a spinster and walked with a cane.

SCENE: SUZANNE *talking to* MISS DAWSON *in her office.*

*(*MISS DAWSON *is a thin, white-haired woman wearing a dark coat sweater. She carries a cane.)*

MISS DAWSON: I have observed you sitting alone behind the dorm. The committee read your notes on T. S. Eliot and Richard Wright. You will not be allowed to re-enter.

SCENE ENDS.

SUZANNE (Present): March 17, 1951, was my last day in the dorm. I was three months pregnant.

My parents were humiliated. My father was a well-known Cleveland minister. They sent me to New York. I stayed with my aunt, my father's sister. She was a music teacher who had never married. She lived in Harlem. Those were the saddest months of my life.

My babies were born the beginning of September in Harlem Hospital, September 2, 1951.

My aunt begged me to stay in New York. I didn't know why but I wanted to return to Columbus. Finally Aunt Louise remembered a friend she had known when she went to Spelman who lived in Columbus. Her friend was Mrs. Tyler, a widow who boarded students in her large house near Long Street.

I took my baby daughters and boarded the train.

Aunt Louise came to Grand Central. She cried.

AUNT LOU'S VOICE: Sue, please stay here.

SUZANNE (Present): But I wanted to return. My parents hadn't spoken to me. But they gave me money. I settled in with Mrs. Tyler. It was agreed I would care for my daughters in the daytime and in the afternoon from four o'clock to nine o'clock I got a job as a department store stock girl. Mrs. Tyler asked me no questions. She knew.

Louise Carter was my aunt. Before my aunt became a music teacher she had had a short career as a singer. She sang in local churches as well as at concerts of Negro groups.

SCENE: SUZANNE *sitting in dimly lit sewing room, holding twins.*

SUZANNE (Present): My twins were three months old when I returned to Columbus.

It had been a year since I had gone to Bobby's

home. I remembered his wall of recordings. He talked about Mozart, one of his favorite books was *Elizabethan World Picture*. He had given me a copy. Often I would meditate on repetitive phrases:

SUZANNE: *(In sewing room.)*
    Chain of being
    Sin
    the Links in the Chain
    the Cosmic Dance

SUZANNE (Present): I had learned he was from New York. I had also learned he had gone to Fordham, and had been married briefly to an Indian woman. It was his first year at Ohio State when I entered his freshman class. He was twenty-nine.

The days were long caring for the babies. Sometimes Mrs. Tyler's neighbors shunned me.

SEWING ROOM SCENE ENDS.

SUZANNE (Present): Iris Ann dropped out of school and went back to Akron. I remembered the early days of my pregnancy and how she had gone to the health center with me. The fall of my sophomore year my major became elementary education. After I received a "C" in the trial course on Wilde and Shaw I was told by the secretary in the English Department that I could take no further English courses. My professor had been a man called Hodgson, a tall man in his fifties. He was accompanied often by his assistant. He smiled a great deal but seldom talked to anyone. He gave me "C's" on every paper. When I told the secre-

tary I'd like to talk to him, she said Professor Hodgson
was not able to see any more students that quarter but I
could make an appointment with his assistant.

So in the fall I declared elementary education and
began taking courses on teaching children. How I
missed the imagery, the marvel, the narratives, the language of the English courses.

The new courses made me depressed. I hated
them.

I ran into Professor Hampshire at the bookstore
on High Street. I told him how hard I had worked on
my papers on Shaw. He suggested I leave one at his office. I went to his office twice before I went to his
house after Christmas.

SCENE: *Dorm room*
　　IRIS ANN *lying across bed.*
　　SUZANNE (1950) *standing by doorway listening to mu-
sic from corridor.*

SUZANNE (Present): Iris Ann had been the only person who
　　knew I was pregnant. She was still sad over Artie and
　　often we cried at night. The white girls gave parties in
　　the dorm.

(Dorm music, Oklahoma.*)*

SUZANNE (Present): But we were never invited. Often they
　　played music from Broadway musicals, *Oklahoma,
　　Carousel.* Iris Ann and I went to the movies.

SCENE ENDS.

SUZANNE (Present): Easter was when I told my father that I had been dismissed from the dorm. He was sitting in the office at his church. Tears came into his eyes.

SCENE: SUZANNE *in the coupe in the stadium holding the twins.*

Now sometimes on Sunday when I thought the campus was empty, I'd put the twins in Mrs. Tyler's coupe and drive to the river or the stadium. Sometimes I'd sit in the stadium inside the car and try to figure out what I was going to do with my life. The twins were in blankets on the seat next to me. I'd hold their fingers and, exhausted, fall asleep.

SCENE ENDS.

SUZANNE (Present): I continued my routine of working as a stock girl.
Finally one February evening I went to one of Bobby's lectures sitting far in the back of the auditorium. It was on King Arthur's death. Bobby read at length in the dimly lit auditorium

SCENE: *Auditorium.* SUZANNE *watches* HAMPSHIRE. *Her appearance has changed. She is thinner and dressed in darker clothes.*

"Till the blood bespattered his stately beard.
As if he had been battering beasts to death.
Had not Sir Ewain and other great lords come up,
His brave heart would have burst then in bitter woe.
'Stop!' these stern men said, 'You are bloodying your-
      self!'
Your cause of grief is cureless and cannot be remedied.
You reap no respect when you wring your hands:
To weep like a woman is not judged wise.
Be manly in demeanor, as a monarch should,
and leave off your clamour, for love of Christ in
      Heaven!
'Because of blood,' said the bold King, 'abate my grief
Before brain or breast burst, I never shall!
Sorrow so searing never sank to my heart;
It is close kin to me, which increases my grief.
So sorrowful a sight my eyes never saw.
Spotless, he is destroyed by sins of my doing!'
Down knelt the King, great care at his heart,
Caught up the blood carefully with his clean hands,
Cast it into a kettle-hat and covered it neatly,
Then brought the body to the birthplace of Gawain.
'I pledge my promise,' then prayed the King,
'To the Messiah and to Mary, merciful Queen of
      Heaven,
I shall never hunt again or unleash hounds
At roe or reindeer ranging on earth,
Never let greyhound glid or goshawk fly.' "

Arthur's only expression of sin in the poem is touched
off by his grief over Gawain. But perhaps it was a battle-sin

of caution, in that but for being "loth to make land across the low water" Arthur would have been at Gawain's side in the battle.

SUZANNE (Present): I didn't know whether Bobby knew anything of what had happened to me. And I had no way of knowing that he was often following me.

AUDITORIUM SCENE ENDS.

AUNT LOU'S VOICE: Forget about that white man.

SUZANNE (Present): Aunt Lou always said:

AUNT LOU'S VOICE: And forget about your parents. I don't know how my brother can ignore his own daughter. But, Sue, I have a little money saved. I'm going to help you go back to school.

SUZANNE: (Present) Seeing Bobby read made me brood over how he had dismissed me. Why?

I often thought of the second course I took with him the winter quarter of my freshman year.

We read *Beowulf*.

He spoke so eloquently of *Beowulf*, then read from it in old English.

Then it happened. Near the beginning of March, Robert Hampshire kidnapped and murdered our daughter. She was the one called Cathi. He drowned her in the ravine.

For a year detectives questioned me. Did I have enemies? Had I ever observed anyone following me?

At that time they didn't ask me about Cathi's father.

Aunt Lou said if they ever did she had a former

student who lived in Mt. Vernon, New York, and she had already discussed it with him. He would be glad to say he was the twins' father.

He was a young man Aunt Lou had helped a great deal and had even loaned him money to start his own cleaners. He was devoted to her.

For a while they seemed to think I knew who the murderer was.

I told him the only odd thing I remembered. Once I had been sitting in the car with my daughters by the river, had for a moment closed my eyes and fallen asleep, and awoke to the sound of someone running away from the car, someone who may have been looking in the window. And I did not drive to the river again.

Then:

SCENE: *Outside the doctor's office. Snow.* SUZANNE *is dressed in a dark coat. The babies lie in white bassinets. She takes the baby through a doorway. The baby coughs violently. She reappears in the falling snow and reaches into the car for the other twin.*
The twin is gone.

SUZANNE (Present): Then there had been a snowstorm. I was worried because Carol had a bad cough and I drove the babies to the doctor's office on Long Street. I pulled the coupe up into a side entrance. The offices were in a large, old-fashioned house. In the heavy snow I pulled the car as close to the door as possible. The babies were in white bassinets. Mrs. Tyler had offered to go with me. But she wasn't feeling well herself. It was snowing hard.

I took Carol into the lobby first and just as I laid her down on the chair she started to cough violently. I held her close. And then laid her back into the bassinet. I told the receptionist I had to get Cathi. I left both the lobby door and the car door open for those seconds. I turned and stepped outside into the falling snow and the few feet to the car. The car door was open, the white bassinet lay on the seat. But Cathi was gone.

SCENE ENDS.

SUZANNE (Present): The detectives felt positive they knew who the murderer was.

Aunt Lou came to Columbus to be with us. I asked her did she think I should get Professor Hampshire to help. "No," she said, "that would serve no purpose." She was the only person who knew Bobby was the father of my girls.

And as far as I know she never told anyone, not even my parents.

For weeks Aunt Lou sat with me in the cold house.

The police would say little but my aunt finally was able to find out that a man called Thurman, who had been in the penitentiary and often walked on campus posing as a student, was suspected. The police told my aunt they felt I knew more than I said and what did she really know about the life I led.

Aunt Lou's Voice (1951): You don't understand. My niece is a sweet girl. A very sweet girl. All you white people are alike. You think because we're Negroes that my niece is mixed up in something shady. My niece knows no Thurman.

Suzanne (Present): She later told me she'd discovered this Thurman had been involved in several petty crimes on campus and in the campus area but also appeared to know many students and told the police he had seen me.

My aunt would not leave me, so in the summer we went back to New York. In the fall I returned to Columbus. I felt my baby's murderer was someone I knew.

(Brief past image of Bunny *and her friends coming along dark corridors giggling.)*

Scene: Suzanne *alone in her dorm room reading Thomas Hardy. From time to time* Bunny *and her friends are heard in the next room singing.*

Suzanne (Present): Why I thought they were capable of murder I don't know but sometimes I suspected a group of girls who lived at the end of the corridor in the dorm. They had been headed by an overweight, dark-haired girl called Patricia "Bunny" Manley. She and her group refused to speak to Iris and me and accused us of stealing her watch from the women's lavatory. If they saw us coming down the corridor they would giggle and close their door. I hated them. Their way of laughing when they saw us coming into the lounge, then refusal to speak was a powerful language. It had devastated me.

And then there had been the watch incident, an incident so disturbing, especially since I myself owned beautiful possessions and jewelry that my parents had given me on going away to school. Both my parents were college graduates (my father, Morehouse, my mother, Atlanta University). I hid in the room and read Thomas Hardy. I loved the language of the landscape.

SUZANNE: *(Still in dorm room.)* "Behind him the hills are open, the sun blazes down upon the fields so large as to give an unenclosed character to the landscape. The lanes are white, hedges low and plashed the atmosphere colorless. Here in the valley the world seems to be constructed upon a smaller, more delicate scale."

SCENE ENDS.

SUZANNE (Present): I remember how I had grown to dread the blocks bound by the stadium, the High Street, the vast, modern, ugly buildings behind the Oval, the dark old Union that was abandoned by all except the Negro students. And too, we were spied upon by the headmistress. She made no secret of the fact that she examined our belongings. "That's our general practice," she said.

Bunny and her friends bragged often to the maids that Iris and I had nothing in common with them, that there was nothing to talk about with us. I felt such danger from them. Had they somehow sought out me and my babies? Of course I told no one this. But I knew whites had killed Negroes, although I had not witnessed it. Thoughts of secret white groups murdering singed the edge of the mind.

I was often so tense that I wound the plastic pink curlers in my hair so tightly that my head bled. When I went to the university health center the white intern tried to examine my head and at the same time not touch my scalp or hair.

"You're probably putting curlers in your hair too tightly," he said, looking away.

Now I remembered my father's sermons on lynching and the photographic exhibits we often had in our church of Negroes hanging from trees.

Then I met David. He would come by and say hello to Mrs. Tyler. When he discovered Carol was my child he made every effort to talk to me. He sensed my sorrow. When he found out that Cathi had been tragically killed he started to come by every evening after he left the law library. He asked no questions but only treated me with such great tenderness.

Finally I told him of everything. My pregnancy, my expulsion, the murder, and how I had returned to Columbus to see if I could find the murderer of my daughter.

I did not tell him yet of Bobby.

In the next months David and I spent many happy hours talking.

The police now referred to Cathi's drowning as the Ravine Murder.

Aunt Lou wrote and still encouraged me to leave Columbus.

By this time David had proposed to me. He was from Washington.

Scene: David *and* Suzanne *sitting in* Mrs. Tyler's *parlor.*

Suzanne (Present): He told me how much I would love his family, particularly his younger sister, Alice, who he said was so much like me. She was studying literature at Howard (read several books at a time) and was also absolutely in love with the movies. He laughingly told me how she wrote brief plays as a hobby and how she'd come home from a movie and get members of her family to act out scenes from them.

He said her favorite movie star was Bette Davis, who she could not only imitate but also had made herself copies of Davis's dresses from *Dark Victory, Now Voyager*, and *The Letter.*

He said she also knew a great deal of poetry and would recite Edgar Allan Poe, Shelley, and Langston Hughes.

He had told her about Carol. And she had already crocheted a white bib for her and was sending it along with butter cookies for us.

Parlor scene ends.

Suzanne (Present): My aunt said I was very lucky.

She encouraged me to look to the future now.

SCENE: *Auditorium, past.*

SUZANNE (Present): I had seen Robert Hampshire. In the bookstore there was a notice that he was again reading from King Arthur. I went.

He seemed far paler and smaller than I remembered. He didn't seem like anyone I had known. He read as usual without looking up from the page. It was clear he felt disdain for the audience. And it was clear he was very agitated.

After he read he spoke of King Arthur and the abyss.

HAMPSHIRE: The abyss in any form has a fascinating dual significance. On one hand it is a symbol of depth in general; on the other a symbol of inferiority. The attraction of the abyss lies in the fact that these two aspects are inextricably linked together. Most ancient or primitive peoples have at one time or another identified certain breaks in the earth's surface or marine depth with the abyss. The abyss is usually identified with the land of the dead, the underworld, and is hence though not always associated with the Great Mother and earth god cults. The association between the netherworld and the bottom of seas or lakes explains many aspects of legends in which palaces or beings emerge from an abyss of water. After King Arthur's death his sword thrown into the lake by his command is caught as it falls and before being drawn to the bottom flourished by a hand which emerges from the waters.

Suzanne (Present): David and I had begun plans to marry. He bought me a ring at Hoensteins.

Many people at Ohio State assumed that Val was the father of my twins. But Val and I never had an intimate relationship. When he discovered I was pregnant he just stopped calling. "I'm surprised," he told Iris Ann. "I really am surprised."

Like my parents he just could not believe this had happened to me. He didn't, like them, really want to know anything further. With my preference for Peter Pan blouses and precise straightened curls I had been almost a cliché of the ultimate virgin. I had totally believed sex was a sin before marriage.

Scene: Mrs. Tyler's *parlor*
Suzanne *and* Val.
Suzanne *holds* Carol *in her arms.*

Suzanne (Present): When Cathi was murdered he came to Mrs. Tyler's.

Val: *(In Mrs. Tyler's parlor.)* Is it true it was your child that was murdered?

Suzanne: Yes.

Val: It's all so difficult to believe.

Suzanne (Present): He had brought me a box of chocolates. For when we had gone out to the freshman parties he often gave me a box of Whitman or Fanny Farmer chocolates.

VAL: Why don't you leave Columbus, Sue?

SUZANNE: I think I can eventually find out who killed my baby if I stay.

VAL: If I were you I'd leave. Most people at State think you left after you got pregnant, they think you went to New York.

SUZANNE (Present): I saw how uncomfortable he was sitting on Mrs. Tyler's stiff couch. I held Carol in my arms. He seemed afraid to look at her.

SUZANNE (1951): *(In Mrs. TYLER's parlor.)* Thank you, Val, for coming by.

SUZANNE (Present): He stood and went to the door. Finally he glanced at Carol, frowned, and left.

VAL: *(In the parlor.)* Good bye, Sue.

SCENE ENDS.

SUZANNE (Present): I often remembered Bunny and her friends had given the illusion of withholding secrets.

I had found a book about symbols on the bottom shelf of the bookstore on High Street. Often on a bottom shelf near the door there were assorted books and portfolios for sale. It was there I discovered several out-of-print soft-cover books on the French Impressionists. I bought one on Cézanne. And hung a print in my room. It was of the port of Marseille. I studied the blues, reds, and yellows. It was the brightest color in the dorm with its dark furniture.

SCENE: SUZANNE, *past, in dorm room reading book of symbols.*

SUZANNE (Present): Bunny and her friends in the closed room next door had become something I thought of a great deal. Their refusal to talk to me made me feel that they knew something about me that was not apparent to myself.

SUZANNE: *(Still in dorm room.)* "Secrets," my book on symbols said, "symbolize the power of the supernatural and this explains their disquieting effect upon most human beings."

SUZANNE (Present): My little book of symbols that I had bought on sale became precious to me.

I remembered again that during the quarter that I had taken the trial course I became very quiet.

SCENE ENDS.

SUZANNE (Present): The police also suspected a neighbor of Mrs. Tyler's, but David, Aunt Louise, and Mrs. Tyler all said it had to be a stranger.

Alice, his sister, David said, was crocheting another bib; this one was pale yellow.

It was spring. Two years had passed since I lived in the dorm.

David and Mrs. Tyler told me every day that all this would be resolved and that one day the police would discover who had followed me in the snow.

Right after Easter Mrs. Tyler told me a grad student from Ohio State was coming that evening. He was doing a study of Negroes in the Columbus area and had heard from campus housing that she kept students and was also a native of Columbus and knew a great deal about the depression years there and the development of the neighborhoods.

When I left she was expecting him for an interview and had made cocoa.

David had gotten me a job in the law library in the stacks. The hours were 6:00 to 9:30. By 10:00 P.M. I was home. We saved money. David worked on two part-time jobs. Aunt Lou gave us something. That evening we pulled the car out of the drive at 5:20 to go to the law library. When we returned at 10:05 the Ohio State murders had occurred.

Robert Hampshire (posing as a researcher) had killed Carol, our twin, and himself. It seems that once inside Mrs. Tyler's living room he told her he was the father of the twins, that he had never been able to forget their existence. They ruined his life. He said he knew that one day I would reveal this, that he would be investigated, there would be tests and his whole career would fail.

He admitted he had waited for me outside the doctor's office and had taken Cathi. He told her he tried to follow the advice of his father who lived near London who had told him to just ignore me but he had been unable to do that. He was quite mad, she said, and had pushed her into the hallway and down the cellar stairs. When her son returned at 8:55 he found her crying and injured on the dark stairwell. Upstairs in the small sewing room where Carol and I slept Robert had killed Carol and himself (with a knife he had taken from the kitchen sink).

SCENE: *Law library, past.*

SUZANNE (Present): David found me here in the stacks of the law library on level zero sorting definitions of words. He remembers . . .

SUZANNE: *(In the law library, past)* Abyss, bespattered, cureless, misfortune, enemy, alien host, battle groups fated to fall on the field today.

SCENE ENDS.

SUZANNE (Present): For many months I made drawings of the corridors in the dorm with the doors of each room outlined in red ink and muttered definitions of rooms, stains, color, skin.

I wrote long passages about my scalp and how it had bled and how I had examined my pores in a magnifying glass. And how the spots on the pillow cases had frightened me so that I had hidden my pillow cases even from Iris Ann.

But it seems the maid in the dorm corridor had told Miss D. that my pillow cases were stained. And they had examined the cloth together.

I thought I would die. David told me years later that he believed I was unable to go on. His parents and sister prepared a room for me in their house in Washington on 16th Street. It overlooked a part of Rock Creek Park. It was Alice's room. She gave it to me. It was a large, pale, cream-colored room with an arch and lovely windows. I didn't leave that room for months.

David and I were married the following year.

I remained in Washington living with his family in the big old house on 16th Street. His father was a lawyer with the NAACP. In a year David finished law school at Ohio State.

The university protected Robert Hampshire for a long time. Nothing of the story came out in the papers. There were stories that a white professor had wandered into the Negro section of Columbus and was killed.

But years later I heard Robert Hampshire's father had come from London at the time. My father, who knew the state politicians, had also put pressure on the papers to bury the tragedy. He convinced them it was best for me.

Mrs. Tyler and her son stuck to the story that a researcher had come to the house, had gone into a fit of insanity, and that was all they knew. Within days the stories were confused.

David, Aunt Lou, and David's family told me nothing. Not even that my mother had been hospitalized.

Before today I've never been able to speak publicly of my dead daughters.

Good-bye, Carol and Cathi.

Goodbye . . .

(Pause.)

And that is the main source of the violent imagery in my work. Thank you.

(Lights bright on hundreds of books in stacks and on the window, falling snow.)

END

The Film Club

(A Monologue by
Suzanne Alexander)

Often when I'm despondent, I watch Bette Davis's movies. Yesterday I started to make a list of them. While I wrote I found myself remembering when my husband, David, was detained in West Africa the winter of 1961. He was missing for fifteen months. Often evenings in Accra David read to me about methods of torture during imprisonment. It was from Fanon:

> "The brutal methods
> which are directed toward
> getting prisoners to speak
> rather than to actual
> torture. There is a mass
> attack . . . "

In that winter of 1961, David's and my life changed. As did Alice's, my sister-in-law's.

Alice and I waited for David in London. I had flown from Accra, she from Washington. We expected David to arrive in London in a week.

I looked at one of Alice's movies today. In remembrance. I call them Alice's movies because it was Alice who formed our film club, in 1959, typed our scripts, directed, and filmed scenes with all of us playing parts. She chose Bette Davis movies. And "adapted" them. She referred to them as "my films." She even sent one to Kazan.

That was also the summer we went to Birdland. Dizzy was there.

I'm sure you know Alice Alexander's poetry and her collections of slave narratives. She died last week of an asthmatic attack in Washington, D.C.

In 1961 we were staying in a room in London at 9 Bolton Gardens, waiting. We had no word from David. I became so distraught that one night I tried to climb into the closed garden to sleep. I developed ailments, nausea, breathlessness. My doctor tried to involve Alice and me in a theatrical reading he was working on with patients. They were doing excerpts from Bram Stoker's *Dracula*. My doctor's name was Freudenberger. He said, "The readings will distract you while you are waiting for your husband."

I read the role of Lucy and Alice read Mina. The doctor lived in the Little Boltons in a dark, damp dwelling. We didn't know it but David was in trouble. Alice filmed our readings as well as us walking on Old Brompton Road.

David and I have written several poems together. We record together and perhaps some of you have seen my most famous play, *She Talks to Beethoven*, a play set in Ghana during David's first disappearance. I also teach the essays of Alice Walker, the poetry of Borges, Lorca, Ishmael Reed, and the plays of Wole Soyinka. Students at New York University are doing an early play of mine. The first line is: "Everyone is reading *Catcher in the Rye*."

In those early days Alice often told me plots of Bette Davis movies. She knew them by heart, as well as the stories of Davis's life. She'd say: In 1930 Bette Davis stepped off a transcontinental train in Hollywood with a six-month contract in hand, a dream of stardom in her head . . . dreams that soon began to fade.

She'd read from a book she'd bought at Marboro's. She'd say: "Kate Bosworth, a young artist, meets a handsome lighthouse inspector, Bill (Glenn Ford), while spending the summer on Martha's Vineyard as the houseguest of her guardian, Mr. Lindley (Charles Ruggles). Kate believes she is in love with Bill and he with her when her identical twin sister, Patricia, shows up and becomes enchanted by Bill.

Patricia and Bill marry. Determined to forget her painting and studies with a cruel but brilliant artist, Kate hears that Bill and Patricia will leave for Chile to live. She decides to give up studying and retreat to the Vineyard house. When she returns to the Vineyard, she discovers Patricia did not go with Bill . . .

. . . For a while Kate pretends to be her twin, Patricia, hoping to gain Bill's love. But one day she decides she cannot go on. And for the final time returns to the Vineyard. But Bill follows Kate to the Island, knowing now she is the sister he should have married . . . "

That winter of 1961 every day we went to the American Embassy for word of David. After we left the Embassy we'd go to Windsor in the rain. Queen Victoria had grieved for Albert there. My husband, where was he? Alice clutched her *Blue Guide* and we went to see the Roman wall in the City.

I remembered in our garden in Accra how David read me the love poems of Senghor.

Now I was expecting our child, Rachel.

Evenings in Accra David had often told me of soldiers who were prisoners. Generally speaking they had a noise phobia and a thirst for peace and affection. Their disorders took various forms, as states of agitation, rages, immobility, many attempted suicides, tears, lamentations, and appeals for mercy.

Alice continued to write David at the American Embassy in Ghana. But we didn't know where he was. She wrote:

"Suzanne wants to return to Africa and search for you. The doctor says she cannot travel back to West Africa. It might kill the baby."

In the rain we take the 30 bus down Old Brompton Road, past the South Kensington station, take another bus and walk into the Haymarket and wait for letters at American Express. And in the afternoon again we go to Windsor.

Suzanne is drawn to the painting of the tiny, sad figure of Victoria dressed in black mourning her husband's death. We walk in Windsor Park until it is dark and we have to take the train back to London. Suzanne's doctor phones. His theatrical group is waiting for us. We read from Stoker:

> ' . . . *All at once the*
> *wolves began to howl as*
> *though the moonlight*
> *had had some peculiar*
> *effect on them. The*
> *horses jumped about and*
> *reared and looked*
> *helplessly round with*
> *eyes that rolled in a way*
> *painful to see; but the*
> *living ring of terror*
> *encompassed them on*
> *every side —* '

Dr. Freudenberger gave me the part of Lucy. These readings were for our amusement and I don't think the others realized how strongly I was affected by the passages I read on Lucy.

I began to utter them in my sleep.

> Lucy sleepwalks to the
> suicide seat on the East
> cliff.
> Dracula drinks her blood
> for the first time.
> She receives a blood
> transfusion.
> The wolf Bersker escapes
> from the zoo, breaks
> a window providing
> Dracula with passage to
> Lucy
> again.
> Lucy dies.
> She is buried in a church
> yard near Hampstead
> Heath."

Dr. Freudenberger sat behind his desk as we read. His nervous German wife, Heike, served tea, sat aside, and studied *Steppenwolf*.

Alice wrote David:

"On the Thames going to Greenwich Suzanne recites one of your favorite poems from Diop. She carries notebooks of your records of slave ships, slave quarters, slaves crouching below the stern on the ship. My husband, she told a stranger, gives lectures on slave ships crossing the Atlantic. We reach Greenwich and see the place where Elizabeth I was born.

"She recites Diop as we cross the grounds up to the observatory. Her breathlessness is worse. And my asthma is bad. Yet she quotes the poem:

> *The Vultures*
> *Way back then with their civilizing edicts*
> *with their holy water*
> *splashing on domesticated brows*
> *the vultures in the shadows*
> *of their claws were setting up*
> *the bloody monument of the*
> *guardian era*
> *way back then*

laughter gasped its last . . .

"Suzanne must leave London, Dr. Freudenberger says, by the beginning of March. Often nauseated, she is in the Haymarket at American Express mornings when the offices are still closed. She doesn't want to leave Europe without word of you. Afternoons she sits by the gas fire and cries. 'Do you trust Dr. F.?' she asks.

"Freudenberger walks us back from the reading along the dark curved street to No. 9, staring at Suzanne.

"In three nights we plan to leave London. Our theatrical group reads sequences that Freudenberger loves.

Jonathan Harker arriving
at Klausenberg stays the
night, leaves by coach for
Castle Dracula . . .
realizes he is a prisoner,
watches Dracula crawl
face down over the castle
wall . . .
enters the forbidden
room . . .
Dracula makes Harker
write three misleading
letters to England . . .

Harker discovers his
personal effects are gone . . .
Dracula leaves the castle
dressed in Harker's
clothes and returns with a
child for the three
vampire women . . .
the bereft mother is killed
by wolves . . .
Harker climbs along the
castle wall to the cellar
where he finds Dracula in
a box.

"These sequences we read sitting in a circle. Sometimes it makes Suzanne cry. We have to leave London with no word from you. Our last day we sailed again on the Thames to Greenwich, returned and went to a movie in Leicester Square."

In three weeks we knew David had disappeared. I went back to Washington and lived with his family. Our daughter, Rachel, was born. David's family says I lapsed into sleeplessness, hysteria. I began to exhibit signs of the prisoners David had described to me, states of agitation, rages, immobility, tears, attempted suicides, lamentations, appeals for mercy.

We heard from the Ghanaian Embassy there was a doctor in Algeria who had once tried to kill Fanon. And this Sottan was behind the plot against my husband. We later learned this Sottan had us followed through the villages in Africa. We remembered an incident at our cottage behind the Ambassador Hotel, a man who said he was the gardener. And earlier on our voyage on the *Elizabeth* there had been a man in the ship's orchestra who had befriended us.

On the last morning in London Dr. Freudenberger and Alice found me wandering along the Embankment near More's Gardens. I thought we were at one of our readings and began to cry the words of Stoker:

> *"When I saw again the*
> *driver was climbing into*
> *the calèche and the*
> *wolves had disappeared,*
> *this was all so strange*
> *and uncanny that a*
> *dreadful fear came upon*
> *me and I was afraid to*
> *speak or move. The time*
> *seemed interminable as*
> *we swept on our way*

now in almost complete

darkness . . . "

My husband, where is he?

Alice wrote that I was delirious and had started to speak of branches of trees cracking together wild roses, mountain ash, lines from Stoker. It was after the birth of our daughter, Rachel.

We read in the *Washington Post*:

"It is believed that

Professor David

Alexander, a native of

Washington and a

graduate of Ohio State

University, was taken to

dinner by a Swiss

journalist in Geneva last

winter, a journalist who

was working for the

French Secret Service.

Alexander, who worked

with Fanon, had been

trying to uncover a plot

against the revolutionary

writer's life. During the
dinner observers say
Alexander became
violently ill after having
an aperitif and was
admitted to the hospital.

Nothing more is
known but it is suspected
he was poisoned with
filicin. His family has
been unable to determine
his whereabouts.

As you may recall,
Fanon died here in
Washington last year.

The Alexanders of
16th Street, N.W. here in
the city have endured
great sorrow this year.
Two months ago the baby
daughter, Rachel, of
Alexander and his wife,
Suzanne, was involved in
an accidental death.

Circumstances are not

known."

After David returned sometimes we walked at night in Rock Creek Park. I reread *Wretched of the Earth* to try to understand what you had been through. Your symptoms:

> *idiopathic tremors*
> *hair turning white*
> *paroxysmal tachycardias*
> *muscular stiffness*
> *anxiety and feeling of imminent death*
> *heavy sweating fits.*

We never got to see Frantz. Alice and I went to the hospital in Washington where we thought he was. We were not admitted.

I still read from his life and search for the cause of his illnesses and death.

My romantic sister-in-law, up until her death we all lived on 16th Street. I see her writing scripts, arranging us all for the camera.

We never had a film club again. After David's imprisonment Alice didn't make films much.

Several years ago at Thanksgiving we looked for

Alice's favorite scene of *Now Voyager*; it was missing. She believed she lost it that winter in London.

I continue to read long passages from Fanon, but for now a brief segment:

> *"But the war goes on:*
> *and we will have to bind*
> *up for years to come the*
> *many sometimes*
> *ineffaceable wounds that*
> *the colonialist onslaught*
> *has inflicted on our*
> *people."*

END

The Dramatic Circle

A radio play commissioned by WNYC, New York City. *The Dramatic Circle* is a dramatization of the events in the monologue *The Film Club*.

PLACE   London, 1961
CHARACTERS
     ALICE ALEXANDER Narrator, a writer and college
teacher
     SUZANNE ALEXANDER Her sister-in-law, a writer
     DAVID ALEXANDER A writer and college teacher, Su-
zanne's husband
     DR. FREUDENBERGER An English doctor
     THE DRAMATIC CIRCLE Dr. Freudenberger's patients
     THE AMBASSADOR

ALICE ALEXANDER: London, 1961. We were staying in Old
     Brompton Road waiting for David to come from
     Ghana.

(Sound of clock striking.)

Suzanne had been delirious the night before, sleepwalking, speaking lines from the historical letters of Napoleon and Josephine. Her breathlessness had become worse.

SUZANNE ALEXANDER: "I can only write you a word at five o'clock in the morning. I have beaten the Russians and taken two cannons and their baggage train and six thousand prisoners. It was raining and we were in mud up to our knees . . . I was worried, the road . . . "

(Sound of footsteps under.)

ALICE ALEXANDER: In the past my brother had written me when he had been traveling with Frantz Fanon, the famous psychiatrist and revolutionary from Martinique. He'd written about the psychiatric cases they had encountered in Algeria. I realized now some of the symptoms of Fanon's patients were like Suzanne's symptoms. She had always missed David when he traveled to do research.

His first trip to Russia had been the summer she found a worn paperback of Napoleon's letters when he was away in battle. I had never seen her as sad as she was that summer that David traveled to Russia and then to France to meet Fanon. David and Suzanne had always traveled together, but now his research on Fanon, the trips the research required, were trips he forbade her to take. He said there was danger surrounding Fanon.

SUZANNE ALEXANDER: "I would like as much to see you, to live quietly, I could do other things but fight, but duty comes before all else. All my life I have sacrificed everything, tranquillity, my own desire, my happiness, my destiny." *(Sigh)*

ALICE ALEXANDER: Often he sent me notes on Fanon's observations, some on Goa.

DAVID ALEXANDER: Even the sky is constantly changing. Some days ago we saw a sunset that turned the robe of heaven a bright violet. Today it is a very hard red that the eye encounters. At Tessalit we cross the French military camps. We must work fast, time passes, the enemy is still stubborn, he does not believe in military defeat but I have never felt victory so possible, so within reach. We only need to march and charge. We have mobilized furious cohorts, loving combat, eager to work. We have Africa with us.

(Music.)

ALICE ALEXANDER: I decided Suzanne had to see a doctor. I found out from a chemist near the South Kensington underground station that National Health was right down the road from us. There were several doctors there. The chemist said, "Dr. Freudenberger is the one I recommend. I think you would find him most sympathetic. I believe he actually went to school in America for a while. He's very insightful. I'm sure he could help your sister-in-law."

(Rain falling.)

We went the next afternoon. It was raining heavily. Suzanne's breathlessness was worse. We sat in the outer office. Then Suzanne was called.

DR. FREUDENBERGER: Mrs. Alexander? Mrs. Alexander, yes. Would you—would you just—would you just come in for a moment?

ALICE ALEXANDER: Freudenberger came to the doorway, he was a dark-haired man, very tall, dressed in a suit. He smiled. Suzanne went inside.

DR. FREUDENBERGER: Mrs. Alexander. Mrs. Alexander, I've examined you and can find no reason in your heart or blood for your breathlessness. I recommend rest, especially since you're expecting a child. Have you been in London long? It says on this form that you're American.

SUZANNE ALEXANDER: I am from Washington, D.C., but my husband and I have been living in West Africa for the last two years.

DR. FREUDENBERGER: And why are you in London?

SUZANNE ALEXANDER: We are waiting for David. He is a writer and professor. He's still traveling. For many months he's been doing research, trying to find the source of Frantz Fanon's illness.

DR. FREUDENBERGER: Oh yes, I know his book, *Black Skin, White Masks.*

SUZANNE ALEXANDER: Yes.

DR. FREUDENBERGER: Are you friends of Fanon's?

SUZANNE ALEXANDER: David has traveled with him in Blida. He's writing Fanon's biography. Fanon is in Washington, very ill.

DR. FREUDENBERGER: You came here ahead of your husband?

SUZANNE ALEXANDER: Yes, the doctor in Accra insisted I start my journey home if I want to have the baby in Washington. My sister-in-law is with me.

DR. FREUDENBERGER: Oh, she came to join you?

SUZANNE ALEXANDER: Yes.

DR. FREUDENBERGER: I see here that you're living in Old Brompton Road.

SUZANNE ALEXANDER: We live on the top floor at Number Nine, in rooms with a green marble fireplace. It overlooks Bolton Gardens. We have not heard from my husband in two weeks.

DR. FREUDENBERGER: You are worried.

SUZANNE ALEXANDER: Every day we got to the American Embassy for word.

DR. FREUDENBERGER: That's the cause of your breathlessness.

SUZANNE ALEXANDER: He was to have arrived last week. We called Accra. They say the last they heard was that he went up country.

DR. FREUDENBERGER: Here, Mrs. Alexander, take this drink. It'll help. It's just valerian.

(African music.)

SUZANNE ALEXANDER: You see, in Blida with Fanon, David saw soldiers who were prisoners. Their disorders took various forms, states of agitation, rages, lamentations. I'm afraid David will be imprisoned. He has enemies. He insists West Africa has not yet achieved independence.

DR. FREUDENBERGER: You work together?

SUZANNE ALEXANDER: We write poems and essays, and we've

been teaching at the University of Legon in Ghana. I want you to meet my sister-in-law, Alice. Alice! Alice!

ALICE ALEXANDER: Suzanne called me into the office.

SUZANNE ALEXANDER: Dr. Freudenberger, this is David's sister, Alice Alexander.

DR. FREUDENBERGER: Hello.

ALICE ALEXANDER: How do you do?

SUZANNE ALEXANDER: She came from Washington to be with me.

DR. FREUDENBERGER: Mrs. Alexander, I'd like to talk to your sister-in-law alone for a moment.

SUZANNE ALEXANDER: I'll wait outside.

DR. FREUDENBERGER: Good, good . . . I'm worried about Mrs. Alexander's health.

ALICE ALEXANDER: Yes, yes. I am very worried too. We're a close family. I forced her to come to you because she seemed almost delirious last night. When I awoke she was sleepwalking. Since we've been in London she has inexplicable dreams of historical characters and speaks as the characters in her sleepwalking. I have written down what she said last night for you to read.

DR. FREUDENBERGER: Oh, thank you.

ALICE ALEXANDER: This is how she began as she walked down the hallway. "When I returned from Martinique to France at the close of 1790 . . . "

SUZANNE ALEXANDER: *(overlapping)* "When I returned from Martinique to France at the close of 1790, I leaped from one revolution in the new world only to encounter it in the old. A November journey across the French countryside to Paris brought me to a capital where violence and terror soon were to dominate the scene. A Paris mob burst into the Bastille with the bloody head of a governor. The next night Napoleon's secret plans for a French attack on Egypt were completed. The campaign would undercut British sea power. I was to accompany my husband as far as Toulon and later join him in Egypt. My husband's fleet of ships of war was spectacular."

(Breathlessness. Sound of ocean.)

DR. FREUDENBERGER: And she does this nightly?

ALICE ALEXANDER: Almost each night since we've not been able to reach David. The characters are in different stages but the themes of separation, violence, and love are always present.

DR. FREUDENBERGER: She is greatly distressed. Are you able to stay with her until Professor Alexander arrives?

ALICE ALEXANDER: Yes. We were to meet here and return to Washington together.

DR. FREUDENBERGER: This sleepwalking and her troubled nerves are not good for her baby. Let me get her. Mrs. Alexander? Mrs. Alexander.

SUZANNE ALEXANDER: Oh, yes.

DR. FREUDENBERGER: Your sister-in-law and I have had a good talk. I was thinking, since you're both here waiting for Professor Alexander, perhaps you'd welcome a little diversion. I'd like to invite you both to my home. My wife and I have a dramatic circle. We're currently reading Bram Stoker's *Dracula*. Readings will distract you both while you're waiting for Professor Alexander.

Suzanne, you could read the role of Lucy, and Alice, you might read Mina. My house is in the Little Boltons.

ALICE ALEXANDER: Very well. Thank you, we are lonely. We know no one here. We're to see a West African writer, but he's in Paris. We will be happy to come to your dramatic circle.

DR. FREUDENBERGER: Lovely. Please come this evening, you're nearby. My wife, Heike, is a translator. She makes tea. We have sherry.

ALICE ALEXANDER: Thank you.

SUZANNE ALEXANDER: Thank you. Good-bye, Dr. Freuden-berger.

ALICE ALEXANDER: Good-bye, Dr. Freudenberger.

DR. FREUDENBERGER: Oh no, please, please. I'm Sebastian.

(Overlapping good-byes.)

ALICE ALEXANDER: As we left I heard Dr. Freudenberger reading the paper I'd given him.

DR. FREUDENBERGER: "My life was transformed. Violence flared savagely when mobs appeared and the court-yards of the Tuileries ran with the blood of Swiss Guards. Danger struck everywhere."

(Music — Wagner chorus. Dramatic circle greetings.)

ALICE ALEXANDER: We arrived at eight for the reading of *Dracula*. Dr. Freudenberger's parlor was small and dark with water-stained gold-and-white wallpaper. His tall wife, Heike, poured tea. Dr. Freudenberger sat behind a large desk, we read from crimson books. He had a giant handwritten script. We later discovered that all the participants were his patients. We read sitting in a circle.

(Music and voices in background.)

Dr. Freudenberger: Ladies and gentlemen, please, everyone. We have two new actors tonight. They're both from America. I've invited them here to join us while they're here in England. In fact, both are writers themselves. Mrs. Alexander, Suzanne, writes essays and plays and Miss Alexander, Alice, writes poetry. So, let us begin.

Dracula, Chapter 15, Dr. Stewart's diary continued: "For a while sheer anger mastered me, it was as if he had, during her life, struck Lucy on the face. I smote the table hard and rose up as I said to him, 'Dr. Helsing, are you mad?' He raised his head and looked at me. And somehow the tenderness of his face calmed me at once. 'Would that I were. My madness were easy to bear compared with truth like this. Oh, my friend, why think you did I go so far round? Why take so long to tell you so simple a thing? Was it because I hate you and have hated you all my life? Was it because I wished to give you pain? Was it that I wanted now so late revenge for that time when you saved my life and from a fearful death?' "

WOMAN: *(Reading)* " 'Oh, no. Forgive me,' said I. He went on."

WOMAN: *(Reading)* "We found the child awake."

DR. FREUDENBERGER: "It had had a sleep and taken some food and altogether was going on well. Dr. Vincent took the bandage from its throat and showed us the punctures. There was no mistaking the similarity to those which had been on Lucy's throat. They were smaller and the edges looked fresher, that was all. We asked Vincent to what he attributed them and he replied that it must have been a bite of some animal, perhaps a rat, but for his own part he was inclined to think that it was one of the bats which are so numerous on the northern heights of London. 'Out of so many harmless ones,' he said, 'there may be some wild specimen from the south of a more malignant species. Some sailor may have brought one home and it managed to escape or even from the zoological gardens a young one may have got loose, or one he bred there from a vampire. These things do occur, you know. Only ten days ago a wolf got out, and was, I believe, traced up in this direction. For a week after the children were playing nothing but Red Ridinghood on the heath. And in every alley on the place until this bloofer lady scare came along. Since then it has been quite a gala time with them. Even this poor little mite when he woke up today asked the nurse if he might go away.' "

(Music, voices.)

ALICE ALEXANDER: After reading *Dracula* we had tea and sherry and listened to music. Dr. Freudenberger pulled his chair next to the divan.

(Piano music, Chopin.)

DR. FREUDENBERGER: Tell me about your teaching in Ghana.

SUZANNE ALEXANDER: Oh, we teach Césaire, the plays of Wole Soyinka, Chinua Achebe, and Richard Wright and many other writers.

DR. FREUDENBERGER: And do you write plays?

SUZANNE ALEXANDER: My most recent play is *She Talks to Beethoven*, a play set in Ghana about a time two years ago when David disappeared.

DR. FREUDENBERGER: He has disappeared before?

SUZANNE ALEXANDER: There were threats against his life and he disappeared to protect me from danger.

DR. FREUDENBERGER: He must love you a great deal.

SUZANNE ALEXANDER: We went to school together as children. We won the state reading contest together.

ALICE ALEXANDER: After tea we read *Dracula* again. Then we started to say good night. Sebastian was once more at Suzanne's side.

DR. FREUDENBERGER: How do you spend your days in London?

ALICE ALEXANDER: Well, we walk all over, in Primrose Hill, Regent's Park, along Charing Cross Road. After we leave American Express we take tours of Trafalgar Square. Yesterday we went to Windsor in the rain.

SUZANNE ALEXANDER: Victoria grieved for Albert there.

ALICE ALEXANDER: In the evenings we return on the tour bus

to Old Brompton Road and sit by the gas fire and write David.

SUZANNE ALEXANDER: Where is he? Where's my husband?

DR. FREUDENBERGER: Suzanne, you must rest. I'll walk you both home, you're just along the road. Perhaps I can help you. I know someone at the American Embassy, I'll ring there tomorrow. Also, another patient's daughter has lived in Ghana for years. I'll talk to her, but, Suzanne, you must not think of returning to Ghana. It might kill the baby. I forbid it.

SUZANNE ALEXANDER: I understand.

DR. FREUDENBERGER: I'll go with you to talk to the American ambassador tomorrow.

(Music.)

SUZANNE ALEXANDER: *(absently)* In our garden in Legon, David read me the love poems of Léopold Senghor, then he'd tell me of the incidents in Fanon's life that he'd written about that day. His notebooks covered Fanon's entire life but always it was Blida that haunted him. He told me, "In Blida with Fanon, I saw soldiers . . . "

(African music.)

DAVID ALEXANDER: *(His voice is heard.)* Generally speaking they had a noise phobia and a thirst for peace and affection. Their disorders took various forms, as states of agitated rages, immobility, and many attempted suicides, tears, lamentations, and appeals for mercy.

berger and his hair had been white. I wanted to think about it and I didn't want Suzanne further upset. Why would Sebastian be in our garden? What was the cause of his changed appearance? Suzanne's mind was not at rest. In the morning she was still agitated and it was raining heavily.

(Sound of rain.)

SUZANNE ALEXANDER: "I cannot pass a day without loving you. I cannot even dream . . . "

ALICE ALEXANDER: I was awakened by the sound of Suzanne's voice reading aloud. She hadn't walked in her sleep that night but now was awake, reading a love letter Napoleon had written Josephine. Reading it and rereading these historical letters seemed to give her strength at a time when . . . there were no letters from David.

SUZANNE AND DAVID ALEXANDER: *(Together)* "Every moment takes me further from you and at every moment I find it harder to bear the separation. You are the ceaseless object of my thoughts. My imagination exhausts itself in wondering what you are doing. If I think of you as sad my heart is torn and my misery increases. Write to me and write at length. Accept a thousand kisses of my love, as tender as they are true. I cannot pass a day without loving you. I cannot even drink a cup of tea without cursing the Army which keeps me apart from the soul of my existence. If I leave you with the speed of the torrential waters of the Rhône, it is only that I may return to you sooner."

ALICE ALEXANDER: I waited a moment before I went to her doorway.

SUZANNE ALEXANDER: How did you sleep?

ALICE ALEXANDER: Well. And you?

SUZANNE ALEXANDER: Well, but I'm concerned about what Sebastian was doing in the garden last night. His hair appeared white.

ALICE ALEXANDER: Now I'm convinced that was not Sebastian but a passerby. It would make no sense. Dr. Freudenberger is a charming friend trying to help us. We're both overwrought. I'm convinced it was someone who resembled him.

SUZANNE ALEXANDER: Perhaps this morning the ambassador will have word of David.

ALICE ALEXANDER: Suzanne was anxious that morning and on the bus to American Express I could not stop her from talking repeatedly about the time David had disappeared in Ghana and how she had news only from her radio.

VOICE ON RADIO: Mr. Alexander is still missing. He traveled with Fanon in Blida. His wife is recovering from an unspecified illness. Alexander was by her side in hospital when he suddenly vanished two nights ago.

SUZANNE ALEXANDER: Vanished.

ALICE ALEXANDER: She relived those moments. I worried about her. The writer we were to meet lived in Chalcot Square. We went to see him, but his wife said he was in Paris. We read that Sylvia Plath lived nearby. One night we saw *Billy Liar* at a theater on Shaftesbury Avenue.

(Music. Voices.)

The next night Dr. Freudenberger sat behind his desk as we read. His nervous German wife, Heike, sat aside studying *Steppenwolf*.

(Dramatic circle voices. Music.)

Dr. Freudenberger hadn't been able to come to the embassy that day. Neither Suzanne nor I mentioned the figure in the garden. Sebastian read the part of Van Helsing.

DR. FREUDENBERGER: "Is it possible that love is all subjective or all objective?"

(Voices reading together.)

"She yet no life taken . . . "

(Dr. Freudenberger alone.)

"Though that is of time and to act now would be to take danger from her forever, but then we may have to warn Arthur, and how should we tell him of this? If you who saw the wounds on Lucy's throat and saw the wounds so similar on the child in the hospital. If you who saw the coffin empty last night and full today with a woman who has not changed only to be more rose and more beautiful in a whole week after she died, if you know of this and know of the white figure last night that brought the child to the churchyard, and yet of your own senses that you did not believe, how then can I expect Arthur, who knew none of those things, to believe? He doubted me when I took him from her kiss when she was dying."

ALICE ALEXANDER: Sebastian read one last passage about Lucy.

DR. FREUDENBERGER: "There lay Lucy seemingly just as we had seen her that night before her funeral. She was, if possible, more radiantly beautiful than ever and I could not believe that she was dead."

WOMAN'S VOICE: "Dead."

DR. FREUDENBERGER: *(Others read along.)* "Her lips were redder than before, and on the cheeks was a delicate bloom."

(Sound of rain.)

ALICE ALEXANDER: Sometimes I wondered if Sebastian thought Suzanne was going to die. Had he told us the truth about her breathlessness? I continued writing my brother letters even though he was missing.

"Dear David,
In the rain we take the 30 bus down Old Brompton Road past South Kensington Station, take another bus at Hyde Park Corner to American Express in hope of a letter from you. We went to Windsor Castle again. Paintings of the sad figure of Victoria seem to comfort Suzanne."

(Dog barking. Footsteps.)

The next night, in the garden, Sebastian seemed to have somewhat changed his appearance. That night his white hair was gone. He limped from one end of the garden to the other, not as the young man he was, but as an old man with a severe ailment. As he limped I felt he knew we were watching although he never looked up.

(Piano, Chopin.)

The ambassador says tomorrow there may be word of David.

(Music. Dramatic circle voices.)

The next reading I still did not mention to Sebastian the figure in the garden, but I did tell him of Suzanne's sleepwalking and her words from her historical letters. He had me recite to him all that I could remember.

"I move against a tragic background but it's clear I not only have a rendezvous with you but one with destiny. Wars have always colored my existence. I was born during the Seven Years' War, and was imprisoned during the French Revolution. Now we are married, my whole life is overshadowed by war. Cannons sound."

Neither of us ever mentioned the garden but I was convinced the figure was Sebastian even though I insisted to Suzanne that it was not . . . New patients joined our dramatic circle, a man from Budapest, a Trinadadian painter.

(Music. Dramatic circle voices.)

The ambassador said we must keep our bags packed, and although he could give us no concrete word, he had learned of some events but could not yet share them. Soon. Suzanne could not stop talking about David's previous disappearance.

At our dramatic circle, we read Stoker as a group.

DRAMATIC CIRCLE: *(Reading together.)* "All at once, the wolves began to howl as though the moonlight had had some peculiar effect on them. The horses jumped about, reared and looked helplessly round with eyes that rolled in a way painful to see. But the living ring of terror encompassed them on every side."

DR. FREUDENBERGER: Suzanne, I would like you to recount the sequences of Lucy's life.

SUZANNE ALEXANDER: Lucy sleepwalks to the suicide seat on the last cliff. *(She reads breathlessly.)*

DRAMATIC CIRCLE: Yes.

SUZANNE ALEXANDER: Dracula drinks her blood for the first time. She receives a blood transfusion. The wolf, Berker, escapes from the zoo, breaks a window providing a passage to Lucy again. Lucy dies.

DRAMATIC CIRCLE: *(After each sentence)* Yes.

SUZANNE ALEXANDER: She is buried in a churchyard near Hampstead Heath. *(Sobbing)*

(Rain.)

ALICE ALEXANDER: The passage made me cry too. We broke the circle then and said good night . . . We continued going to the embassy each morning. The ambassador said we would be leaving London soon. We sailed to Greenwich on the Thames. One afternoon we saw a Bergman movie. Sebastian came again in the middle of the night. That time, just as he left through the gate he seemed to look up at our window . . . I wrote David.

"On the Thames to Greenwich Suzanne recites one of your favorite Diop poems. She carries notebooks of your records of slave ships. Slave quarters, slaves crouching below the stern of the ship. My husband, she told a stranger . . ."

(African music.)

SUZANNE ALEXANDER: My husband gives lectures on the slave ships that crossed the Atlantic.

ALICE ALEXANDER: We reach Greenwich and see the place where Elizabeth I was born. Suzanne recites Diop as we cross the park up to the observatory.

SUZANNE ALEXANDER: "Way back then, with their civilizing edicts, with their holy water splashed on domesticated brows, the vultures in the shadows of their claws were setting up the bloody monument of the guardian era. Way back then laughter gasped its last."

(Telephone rings.)

ALICE ALEXANDER: Finally the ambassador said there was word. We went to Grosvenor Square.

AMBASSADOR: Mrs. Alexander, sit down please. May I get you some coffee?

SUZANNE ALEXANDER: No. No, thank you. Have you heard from David?

ALICE ALEXANDER: Yes, what's the news?

AMBASSADOR: You'll see him tomorrow morning. I spoke to Alexander a few hours ago. He is fine.

ALICE ALEXANDER: Thank God.

SUZANNE ALEXANDER: Are you sure he's all right?

AMBASSADOR: Yes. Last week we knew a few details but I didn't want to talk to you until I was sure of your husband's, and your's brother's, freedom.

SUZANNE ALEXANDER: Freedom?

ALICE ALEXANDER: Freedom? He's been imprisoned?

AMBASSADOR: Yes. But please assure yourself, he is fine now. Let me explain. We have finally heard from our sources that there was a doctor in Algeria who had once tried to kill Fanon, a man named Sottan. And this same Sottan is behind a plot against your husband. We have also learned that this Sottan had you and your husband followed through the villages. There may have been a man who was your gardener at the cottage behind the Ambassador Hotel. And earlier there may have been a man with the ship's orchestra when you were on the *Queen Elizabeth*.

ALICE ALEXANDER: But is he all right?

SUZANNE ALEXANDER: How long was David detained?

ALICE ALEXANDER: How long was my brother in prison?

AMBASSADOR: I don't know. I'm afraid you should know that there has been a rumor that there may have been an attempt to poison him with a drug called filicin. There were rumors that he became violently ill after having an aperitif with a Swiss journalist and was hospitalized. It was at that time we made our connection. But I talked to David this morning and he sounds fine. And he will arrive at Gatwick in the morning at 8:10. I want to assure you, he sounded fine. You will all leave Heathrow at 2:35 in the afternoon, Pan American, he asks that you be ready. And one final note: In the morning there will be an article in the *Herald Tribune* that Frantz Fanon has died in a hospital in Washington, D.C. I'm terribly sorry.

SUZANNE ALEXANDER: No, no.

(Crying. Piano music.)

ALICE ALEXANDER: We hardly felt like going to the dramatic circle, but we went. We knew Sebastian would be disappointed. Instead of scenes, he had us read a litany of dramatic events. He seemed to have a purpose in doing this.

DR. FREUDENBERGER: "Jonathan Harker, arriving at Klausenberg, stays the night, leaves by coach for Castle Dracula."

WOMAN'S VOICE: "Realizes he is a prisoner."

DR. FREUDENBERGER: "Watches Dracula crawl, face down, over the castle wall."

WOMAN'S VOICE: "Enters the forbidden room."

WOMAN'S VOICE: "Dracula makes Harker write three misleading letters to England."

DR. FREUDENBERGER: "Harker discovers his personal effects

are gone. Dracula leaves the castle dressed in Harker's clothes and returns with a child for the three vampire women."

WOMAN'S VOICE: "The bereft mother is killed by wolves."

DR. FREUDENBERGER: "Harker climbs along the castle wall to the cellar, where he finds Dracula in a box."

ALICE ALEXANDER: Then he read the last section.

DR. FREUDENBERGER: "When I looked again, the driver was climbing into the calèche and the wolves had disappeared. This was all so strange and uncanny that a dreadful fear came upon me and I was afraid to speak or move. The time seemed interminable as we swept on our way now in almost complete darkness."

ALICE ALEXANDER: He reached out and held Suzanne's hand, staring at her. We returned to our rooms for the last night at Old Brompton Road and finished packing. Even though the ambassador had said David sounded fine, of course we were very fearful. Three weeks ago we had arrived in London happy and everything had changed. I forced Suzanne to go to sleep and then I went out into the garden and waited for Sebastian's arrival. He came a little before midnight. I ran toward him.

(Steps.)

Sebastian, why have you walked in the garden at night, limping, hair white, almost as an apparition?

DR. FREUDENBERGER: I wanted to appear as an apparition.

ALICE ALEXANDER: But why?

DR. FREUDENBERGER: To prepare Suzanne's mind for the

darkness I knew she must face. The moment I met Suzanne I fell in love with her. As a matter of fact, I'd seen both of you before you came to my office, in a restaurant next to the South Kensington underground station. It was a Sunday. I was struck by Suzanne's fragile beauty. I followed you along the road. I had a premonition that David, like Jonathan Harker, was going through bad times and she, like Lucy, would become the victim of an unfair, tragic plot. I'd hoped that my dramatic circle would help her and you on this difficult journey.

ALICE ALEXANDER: So, David will be changed.

DR. FREUDENBERGER: Yes. But he will recover.

ALICE ALEXANDER: Sebastian kissed me and disappeared before I could even thank him. We never saw our friend again. As the ambassador had told us, in the *Herald Tribune* was the article on Fanon's death . . . We arrived at Gatwick early and waited in the hall behind a glass partition for visitors from Africa. Suzanne had worn David's favorite dress, white silk with a kinte cloth sash. I hardly recognized David, he had changed so. He limped like an old man and his black hair had turned white. Suzanne ran toward him.

(Sounds of terminal.)

SUZANNE ALEXANDER: David!

ALICE ALEXANDER: It was hard to tell at first if he even recognized her. Finally he smiled, they kissed and embraced.

DAVID ALEXANDER: I wanted to see Frantz before he died to

tell him of things I had discovered. We'll have to continue to live by his words.

"But the war goes on and we will have to bind up for years to come the many, sometimes ineffaceable, wounds that the colonialists have inflicted on our people."

(Voices in terminal.)

ALICE ALEXANDER: We helped David through the terminal. In months to come he would recover. The book on Fanon would be powerful, but for now he was lost in Blida.

(Voices increase. African music.)

END

Adrienne Kennedy began to write and have her plays produced in the 1960s. She has been commissioned to write plays for the Public Theater, Jerome Robbins, The Royal Court, the Mark Taper Forum, and Juilliard. Kennedy has been a visiting lecturer at many universities, including Yale, Princeton, Brown, the University of California at Berkeley, Stanford, and Harvard. Kennedy's plays have been part of college curricula in the United States, Europe, and Africa. Her 1964 Obie Award-winning play, *Funnyhouse of a Negro*, was broadcast by the BBC and Radio Denmark, and has been translated into several languages. Kennedy is one of five playwrights included in *The Norton Anthology of American Literature*, third edition, volume 2. **Alisa Solomon** is a free-lance journalist and theater critic living in New York.

DATE DUE

APR 15 1998	
APR 30 1998	